OPPOSITIONAL VOICES

OPPOSITIONAL VOICES

Women as Writers and Translators of Literature in the English Renaissance

Tina Krontiris

London and New York

First published 1992
by Routledge
11 New Fetter Lane, London EC4P 4EE

Simultaneously published in the USA and Canada
by Routledge
a division of Routledge, Chapman and Hall, Inc.
29 West 35th Street, New York, NY 10001

© 1992 Tina Krontiris

Set in 10/12pt Palatino by Selectmove
Printed and bound in Great Britain by
T J Press (Padstow) Ltd, Padstow, Cornwall

British Library Cataloguing in Publication Data
Krontiris, Tina
Oppositional voices: women as writers and translators of literature in
the English Renaissance.
1. English literature. Authors. Women, history, 1485–1603
I. Title
820.99287

Library of Congress Cataloging in Publication Data
Krontiris, Tina
Oppositional voices: women as writers and translators of literature in
the English Renaissance/Tina Krontiris.
p. cm.
Based on the author's Ph.D. thesis.
Includes bibliographical references and index.
1. English literature – Early modern, 1500–1700 – History and
criticism. 2. English literature – Women authors – History and
criticism. 3. Women and literature – England – History – 16th
century. 4. Women and literature – England – History – 17th
century. 5. Women – England – History – Renaissance, 1450–1600.
6. Translating and interpreting – England – History. 7. Authorship
– Sex differences.
I. Title.
PR113.K7 1992
820.9'9287'09031 – dc20   91–14010

ISBN 0–415–06329–9

To the memory of my brother,
Panagiotis Krontiris

CONTENTS

LIST OF FIGURES

ACKNOWLEDGEMENTS

While I worked on this book and the Ph.D. thesis on which it is based, several people offered me moral and material support. I wish to thank them here. I acknowledge with great pleasure the encouragement and materials (books, papers, ideas) I received from Ann Rosalind Jones. If it were not too banal to speak of models nowadays, I would say that she is the model of sisterhood. I would also like to thank Jonathan Dollimore, who supervised the doctoral thesis; his comments on the various chapters were particularly useful. Not least, I must acknowledge the contribution of Betty Travitsky, who patiently answered many queries regarding primary material.

Several other people contributed in various ways. Jina Politi, Peter Stallybrass, Maria Mitchell, and Ania Loomba offered advice or ideas in the beginning stages of my research; my friends Kiki, Asha, Erwin, and (sometimes) Pantelis provided moral support; in Thessaloniki, Stavros Rammos taught me something about textual pleasure. The staff of the Sussex University Library, especially Jenny Marshman and the people in interlibrary loans, were very helpful. Mr James Lund of the University of London, International Hall, helped me with accommodation during my long visits to the British Museum.

English Literary Renaissance granted permission to reprint 'Breaking barriers of genre and gender,' which appeared in volume 18 (1988), and the University of Massachusetts Press similarly allowed me to make use of my essay 'Style and gender in Elizabeth Cary's *Edward II*,' originally published in *The Renaissance Englishwoman in Print*, ed. Anne Haselkorn and Betty Travitsky, 1990. I thank them kindly. Finally, I must acknowledge the financial support of the Greek State Scholarship Foundation between 1984 and 1987.

Tina Krontiris

1

CULTURE, CHANGE, AND WOMEN'S RESPONSES

When Virginia Woolf's *A Room of One's Own* was published in 1929 virtually nothing was known about women writers of the early modern period in England. The general silence on early female literary activity led Woolf to suppose that there were no women who wrote in that period. Woolf had to invent the fictional figure of 'Shakespeare's Sister' in order to explain the historical conditions that obstructed women's creative energy. Since then, thanks to the painstaking work of feminist researchers and to theoretical developments in English and feminist studies, much light has been shed on the living conditions and literary products of early modern women.[1] Today we have a much clearer picture of what these women wrote and what sorts of themes and genres they dealt with. Now we also know more about the precise forms of oppression they were subjected to and why they were unable to write more in an age when, as Virginia Woolf put it, 'every other man, it seemed, was capable of song or sonnet.'[2] Yet it still remains to be seen how they were able to write at all in such an oppressive environment and what effect that environment had on what they finally produced. How is it that the same culture which produced a prohibitive ideology also produced the possibility of even a few women writing, publishing, and sometimes voicing criticism of their oppressors? My overall purpose here is to try to answer this question and to point out the types of ideas women writers contest.

One of the assumptions I work with in this book concerns the relation of theory to fact. I take theory to be not necessarily or not always consonant with actual human behaviour; what happens at the level of social practice is often at variance

1

with specific theories or rules about what should happen. I also assume that ideology in general is not a set of ideas and values which are made by those in power and which remain there unalterable and eternal. Ideological and cultural formations are changing processes; and they are contradictory in character because they are determined by competing social groups of divergent interests.[3] I accept, therefore, that there is a dialectical relationship between women and men in a culture where the imbalance of power is grossly in favour of the latter. In such a situation women are a subordinate group but they are also participants in social change. Change of any sort, that is, is not something that occurs outside the realm of women. Though within western society women have historically possessed much less cultural and political power than men have, they are not for that reason to be thought of as passive and obedient performers of rules dictated from above. The process of internalization may account for the actions of many women, but not of all women. Nor is resistance to be conceived solely in terms of a revolutionary movement. Resistance to oppression can take the form of dialectical relationships within systems of power. 'Resistance to power does not have to come from elsewhere to be real,' Foucault states; 'nor is it inexorably frustrated through being the compatriot of power. Resistance exists all the more by being in the same place as power.'[4]

In her ground-breaking and now classic essay, 'Did women have a Renaissance?'[5] the late Joan Kelly-Gadol answers the question of her title with an unequivocal no. Using mainly material on courtly love from medieval to Renaissance times, Kelly-Gadol argues that as Europe moved from a feudal to an early modern state, women faced new restrictions and stricter codes of subordination. Her view gained wide acceptance, especially on account of its challenge of a common periodization for men and women. Many scholars, especially within feminism, confirmed her view that the period of 'rebirth' meant something very different for each of the two sexes. Today, however, historians and researchers hesitate to accept the view of a complete Dark Ages for Renaissance women and to embrace unqualifyingly Kelly-Gadol's generalizations, as more and more diversified evidence turns up. Margaret Ferguson and the other editors of *Rewriting the Renaissance* seem to voice this recent tendency when they state that 'it is still too early for a definitive answer to Joan Kelly-Gadol's famous question.'[6] While still steering a course directly opposite to Burckhardt's classic assertion that Renaissance women 'stood on a footing of perfect equality with men,'[7] recent historians and researchers increasingly draw our attention to facts about Renaissance women's behaviour in real life and the discrepancy between the private and the public image. Mary Ellen Lamb, for example, examines the translations and correspondence of the Cooke sisters and notes a great difference in the way they appear in their sealed letters and in the prefaces and dedications that accompany their published translations.[8] Judith Brown studies records on the working women in Tuscany and concludes that a large number of women of that area participated in the labour force despite guild regulations against it. On the basis of the information she has uncovered, Brown challenges the generalization of a direct relation between a decline in women's economic status and the development of capitalism made by earlier studies of women's labour, including Alice Clark's *Working Life of Women in the Seventeenth Century*. Brown correctly states:

> Surely the importance of ideology cannot be denied. Renaissance women had to contend with it. But if the rules that constrained their behaviour closed off many options, they still left others open, and . . . women were very inventive in carving out for themselves meaningful, productive, and creative roles. We need, therefore, to look not only at the rules of society but also at how men and women understood them, and often circumvented them.[9]

SIXTEENTH-CENTURY DEFINITIONS OF FEMININITY

The beginning of the sixteenth century witnessed great changes in the political, socio-economic, and religious structures. The umbrella term 'Renaissance,' commonly used for the years roughly between 1500 and 1640 in England, belies these changes; for this reason historians today tend to employ the more accurate term, 'early modern period.' In this book I shall use both terms. In so far as it is a study of women's writing (that is, of an intellectual activity), the word 'Renaissance' produces ironic reverberations because the so-called 'rebirth' in thought and learning does not apply equally to the female half of the population. I use the term 'early modern period' at other times precisely to focus on those changes which affected – differently – the everyday lives of men and women.

In England, as in the rest of Europe, the king consolidates his power and the court becomes a centre for political and cultural activity. In the course of the sixteenth century, courtiership becomes a new profession, and competition for the monarch's favour becomes the norm at court. In the social sphere there is an unprecedented degree of class mobility, both downward and upward, resulting in the expansion of the middle class. Between the two extremes of the highest and the lowest ranks there is a group of craftsmen, tradespeople, and professional men that is getting larger and larger as England's economic position improves and trade becomes a promising enterprise. New opportunities come up, mainly for men. Largely, women are forced out of the business sector and become confined to the private sphere of the home.[10]

In the area of religion, the Reformation is gradually gaining ground as a new major movement. Seeking to increase its ranks, it appeals for support to both men and women. Protestant reformers stress the democratic principle of the religious change in the doctrine of the priesthood of all believers: not only men but women and the low born, in spiritual equality, will be given the right to read and interpret the scriptures. Many of these promises will later be retracted, but meanwhile they work their way, and literacy is encouraged. In the intellectual sphere, humanism brings in the influence of classical thought (Greek and Roman) and emphasizes man's control over his actions and behaviour. A number of liberal early humanists (including More, Vives, Elyot, and Hyrde) attempt to elevate woman and retrieve her from the low status into which she was cast by medieval Christian doctrine. In the family scene there is no great change, though here we must speak more cautiously. Lawrence Stone has claimed a major shift from an open lineage to a nuclear-type family for the late sixteenth century, but more recent historians argue convincingly that by the sixteenth century the English family is already nuclear in structure (consisting of the couple and their children), at least for the majority of the population.[11] Nevertheless, the movements outlined above do not leave the family unaffected. The roles of

4

the husband and the wife are redefined and new ideals and purposes are set for the marriage.

Both humanists and reformers adopted the idea that marriage is not simply for procreation and the avoidance of sin and fornication but also for mutual comfort and companionship. Both aimed to elevate the role of marriage, defending it against celibacy, which was now cast as inferior. The advantages of marriage were elaborated on and married life was praised. In his *Book of Matrimony* (1560), for example, Thomas Becon presents marriage as an ideal, a means to domestic bliss.[12] The elevation of marriage went hand in hand with the elevation of motherhood. Both humanists and reformers joined voices in praising the new mother. Motherhood was now seen partly as a way of saving woman from her original sin, and partly also as an important means in securing the Reformation. Both humanists and reformers, however, charged the husband with the responsibility of supervising the religious and moral conduct of his wife and children. It is in fact this stress on the responsibility of the husband which distinguishes the patriarchy of the post-Reformation period from earlier patriarchies.[13]

Related to these changes, as well as to notions of womanhood inherited from the Middle Ages, are the new requirements for feminine conduct propagated in the course of the sixteenth and early seventeenth centuries. The woman is seen increasingly as a means of guaranteeing family property and honour. Accordingly, female passive qualities are emphasized, especially that of chastity. In the many male-written manuals and conduct books, women are repeatedly warned about the dangers of sexual transgression. Sexual purity is linked to a woman's speech. The quality of silence is not as universally required as chastity, but it is one of the principal virtues in dominant discourse. One English writer declares:

> A womans Tongue that is as swift as thought,
> Is ever bad, and she herself starke Nought:
> But shee that seldome speakes and mildly then,
> Is rare Pearl amongst all other Women.
> Maides must be seene, not heard, or selde or never,
> O may I such one wed, if I, wed ever.[14]

Altogether, woman was seen in terms of her function as a wife and mother, not as a human being with needs and desires of her own. Voicing opinion in public or participating in male activities was usually forbidden. The early humanists, whose views shall be discussed more extensively later, argued in favour of female education, but even they confined women to private roles. Louis Vives, author of the influential treatise *Instruction of a Christian Woman* (translated by Hyrde in 1529), states on the pursuits of a woman:

> the study of wysedome: the which dothe instruct their maners and enfurme theyr lyvyng and teacheth them the waye of good and holy lyfe. As for eloquence I have no great care, nor a woman nedeth it nat: but she nedeth goodness and wysedome.[15]

In his treatise Vives makes it quite clear that the purpose of all instruction for a woman is to make her a virtuous and wise wife, not a competitor in her husband's public world. Sir Thomas More himself, arguably the most liberal of the early humanists, disapproves of a woman writing for public consumption. In one of his letters to his daughter Margaret he characteristically states:

> Content with the profit and the pleasure of your conscience, in your modesty you do not seek for the praise of the public, nor value it overmuch even if you receive it, but because of the great love you bear us, you regard us – your husband and myself – as a sufficiently large circle of readers for all that you write.[16]

In the later part of the Renaissance there appears to be a tightening in the prescriptions. An emergent current of Puritan patriarchalism is partly responsible for this. According to patriarchalist theory, all governing authority is paternal. Both in the commonwealth and the family (the one being analogous to the other) the king/father rules over his subjects.[17] Even queens come under attack from hard-core patriarchalists like John Knox.[18] The tightening of the restrictions has probably something to do also with a reaction to an increase in women's actual opportunities, a topic I discuss later on. Whatever the reasons, later theorists on women's conduct are quite emphatic and restrictive in specifying the requirements for proper feminine conduct. The link between speech and chastity is reinforced. Richard Brathwait, in *The English Gentlewoman* (1631), states:

'What is spoken of Maids may be properly applied to all women: they should be seene and not heard.'[19] The requirements are particularly severe for the wife. Thus Robert Snausel in *A Looking Glasse for Married Folkes* (1631) stresses the threat of a woman's speech to the marriage, and Gervase Markham in *The English Huswife* (1615) goes so far as to forbid her to speak even on matters of faith. The wife's inferiority and subordination to the husband is also stressed. Some theorists and moralists, like William Gouge, require the wife to show outward signs of her husband's superiority (for example, bowing in his presence).[20] Most theorists either take it for granted or specify that one of the wife's duties is to accept her husband's superiority and her own inferiority. The woman instructs her daughters and female servants, but the man is the ultimate authority, the owner, the instructor.[21] One of the husband's duties, derived from Christian doctrine, is to rule. (God conferred upon man, in the figure of Adam, the headship in marriage because man surpasses the woman in strength of body and mind and is thus better suited for the government of wife and household.) 'He may rule with kindness or severity but there must be no question that he rules.'[22] Although many writers on marital conduct urged the husbands to reason with their wives and not to abuse them, they simultaneously forbade the wife to question her husband's authority. If he did abuse her, she ought to forbear. The consolation that some theorists offered was that if she was not rewarded on earth, she would be rewarded in heaven and that heavenly reward would be greater in proportion to her earthly suffering.[23] The patient Griselda, the personification of ideal subservience in women, was frequently proffered as a model. The woman was to derive gratification from the performance of her wifely duty alone.[24]

Such were the theories propounded. What was the relation of these theories to what was happening in the actual lives of women? It is hard to say with certainty. Available documentary evidence (wills, diaries, etc.) has not been systematically read from the women's point of view and sometimes historians base their claims, unproblematically, on literary evidence. But many agree on the discrepancy between theory and practice in this matter. Keith Wrightson thinks that the husband–wife and father–daughter relations were not as authoritarian as moralistic advice leads us to believe, and that in *private* life there existed a companionate ethos, 'side by side with, and often overshadowing, theoretical adherence to the doctrine of male authority and *public* [*sic*] female subordination.'[25] Keith Thomas also agrees that in actual life Renaissance women's independence was greater than theory allowed, 'and part of the evidence lies in the very frequency with which that independence was denounced.'[26] Often conservative formulations reflect the patriarchy's fears and anxieties about losing control over women and they are therefore reactions to, rather than indications of, developing tendencies in the culture. The language in which some of the prohibitions are couched suggests as much. When Powell in *Tom of All Trades* (1631) tells the parents, 'in stead of reading Sir Philip Sidney's *Arcadia*, let them read the grounds of good huswifery,'[27] his advice can only make sense if young girls were actually reading the romance he mentions. Likewise, when Gouge forbids young married couples to use pet names, like 'duck,' 'chick,' and 'pigsnie,' on account that they might induce great familiarity between the partners and hence undermine the husband's authority, we can infer that enough people were in the habit of calling each other by such names to necessitate a warning against their use. It would be more illuminating and useful, therefore, if we paid attention also to other aspects of the system and the processes that allowed women room for self-expression. Since this is a study of female assertiveness in the literary field, I shall take some of the major events and ideologies outlined above in order to show how various contradictions and deflections in change created opportunities for women in the intellectual and public spheres.

THE CONTRADICTIONS OF IDEOLOGY AND THE PARADOXES OF CHANGE

From its very beginnings the Reformation incorporated a fundamental contradiction: it granted woman relative autonomy in spiritual matters but simultaneously endorsed her overall subordination to the husband. Through its doctrine of the priesthood of all believers, it recognized women's right to read and interpret the scriptures, and even to disagree with men in their interpretations. Neither sex nor social rank was to be a barrier in the communication with God. Women could congregate, debate the scriptures, and even preach. The democratic principle was to apply also to matters of morality. In the case of adultery, for example, the man would be punished as severely as the woman. At the same time, however, the Reformation supported male authority and advocated female subordination. William Tyndale, for example, wrote that the woman had to accept orders from her husband as though they were from God.[28] This was the conservative element which eventually led to a retraction of the original position. Conservative reformers began to fear that they were losing control over women and that loss of control would be interpreted by their opponents as a failure of masculine strength. 'They'll say we are being ruled by women,' wrote a pastor to Calvin.[29] Conservatives reacted by tightening the strings. They persecuted women dissident preachers even within the communities which had encouraged freedom in thought and action[30] and emphasized the woman's duty to obey her husband and accept him as spiritual leader. Thomas Becon, one of the conservative reformers, said that women should keep silent in church and ask religious guidance only from their husbands at home, while Hugh Latimer, a conservative preacher, warned husbands to keep constant vigilance over their wives, who, like Eve, might use their feminine wiles to usurp authority in the family.[31]

But once the change had started in a certain direction its course could not be easily reversed. Once the statement of spiritual equality had been broadcast, it could be deployed as a strategy of legitimation. Furthermore, women could benefit from that faction of the Reformation which sought to teach them literacy rather than to take their Bibles away altogether. Indeed, Thomas Becon, the same Protestant enthusiast who advocated woman's silence in church and subordination to the husband at home, was also in favour of female education as a means to fighting idolatry. He proposed a comprehensive and radical plan which involved a secondary school system for girls, comparable, though not equal, to the grammar school for boys: 'If it be thought convenient, as it is most convenient, that schools should be erected and set up for the right education and upbringing of the youth of the male kind, why should it not also be thought convenient that schools be built for the godly institution and virtuous bringing up of the youth of the female kind?'[32] The plan Becon proposed, which would have revolutionized basic education for women, was not finally put into effect, but the voicing of such ideas was advantageous to women, who could in turn appropriate them for other purposes.

Women did apparently exploit the contradictions in Protestant ideologies as well as the unsettlement of the religious situation itself. First, religion could be used by women as a permission to speak. Religion actually creates one of the paradoxes of the sixteenth century: on the one hand women were enjoined to silence while on the other they were permitted to break that silence to demonstrate their faith and devotion to God. In the name of the word of God, women could and did claim their right to speak independently from men. They wrote, translated, and published many religious works. Religion probably prevented many women from writing on secular subjects, as most female authored material in this period consists of religious compositions and translations.[33] None the less, religion gave them a legitimate voice and an opportunity to be heard. Telling about God's word became a sign of breaking the silence and often of disagreeing with men. Even women who worked alongside patriarchalists could assert this as a right. Anne Locke, for example, who left England and her husband to work with John. Knox on the continent, wrote in the dedication of her translation of the *Markes of the Children of God*:

> Because great things by reason of my sexe, I may not doe, and that which I may, I ought to doe, I have according to my duety, brought my poore basket of stones to the strengthening of the wals of that Jerusalem, whereof (by Grace) we are all both Citizens and members.[34]

Thus religion could grant women a voice. Recusant or denominational religious activity could also teach them how to be critical of the established religion and how to fight against it. Most people who disagreed with the official religious dogma kept the matter to themselves or within their own homes; others sought ways to express their dissent. In the case of women, dissidence or departure from the official religion often meant insubordination and refusal to subject oneself to the husband's authority. Anne Askew, a Protestant in the time of Henry VIII, defies men in the name of God and becomes a rebel in the cause of her faith. 'Confronting the priests of Lincoln, seeking

10

to divorce her husband, journying alone to London, and defying the male authorities of the Church and state were all acts by which she defined herself as a true Christian woman, one who could not accept her society's injunctions to be obedient and silent.'[35]

In later times, when Protestantism had become the established religion in England, many women aligned with Catholicism and risked persecution. Elizabeth Cary, whom I discuss later in this volume, is one example. In the name of God she assumes her right to convert, even at the cost of alienating her husband, then Lord Deputy of Ireland and an agent in the suppression of Irish Catholics. Conversion to Catholicism jeopardized her husband's career and embarrassed him in the eyes of the king. Still other women who sought a more active participation turned to sectarian activity. The sects offered them the opportunity for precisely those intellectual and social activities, like preaching, which orthodox religion had denied them.[36] During the reign of Elizabeth, several sects had sprung up and the followers of these sects emigrated to Holland or America, or stayed in England and went underground, meeting clandestinely at conventicles until they reappeared openly in great numbers in the early days of the Long Parliament. Although the overall number of the sects was never great, it is significant that the number of women in them was proportionally large.[37] Among those who gathered in illegal assemblies the women probably outnumbered the men. Also, women tended to associate themselves with the more radical reform groups.[38] The principle of spiritual equality which the Reformation had promised but had not in reality carried to its end was preached as well as practiced by the sects which appealed to women for that reason. Those who joined believed and declared that the spirit of God was to be revealed 'as soon to his hand maids as his men servants.'[39] The sects also allowed women to participate in church government and to preach. They recognized women as spiritually autonomous, independent of their husbands. This was a radical idea which eventually led to a re-examination of the nature and purpose of the family.[40] Open sectarian activity, including preaching by women, took place when the sects returned to England in the early 1640s and hence falls chronologically outside the period of this study, but sectarian ideas had been in circulation much earlier, especially since some sectarian activity had gone underground in London, and communication with the sects in Holland was not infrequent.

Like reformed religion, humanist thought regarded the female sex with a contradictory principle: woman is by nature man's inferior, but through proper training and education she can be brought to approximate his level. Yet in this case it was not only the contradiction within humanist thought that worked in favour of women but also the fact that humanism posited itself as an alternative to a number of well-established conservative discourses and practices – religious, philosophical, medical, legal – which viewed woman's nature not only as inferior but also as fixed.[41] As an ideology of correction through education, humanism created what Lisa Jardine calls cultural confusion[42] but what might perhaps more accurately be termed divergence. Humanist influence in the field of women's education was therefore important not because aristocratic families would educate their daughters according to the model of Sir Thomas More; indeed the model failed if we judge from the small number of women who received advanced classical education after the mid-sixteenth century.[43] Rather, humanist ideas on education became important because they fractured the influence of conservative ideologies. The early humanists had advocated a specific programme of study that included such subjects as religion, moral philosophy, and the classics, aiming to make woman a better wife and mother. Later in the century, Mulcaster (*Positions*, 1581) defended women's education on general humanist principles but avoided specific formulations, voicing instead a certain flexibility and pragmatism: 'I allow them learning with distinction in degrees, with difference of their calling, with respect to their ends.'[44] More conservative men, represented by influential writers like Thomas Salter, translator of Giovanni Bruto, were sceptical about whether women should be educated at all. Fearing loss of control and suspecting that books would induce moral degeneration and scorn for low occupations, these conservatives tried to dissuade parents from educating their daughters. In *A mirrhor mete for all mothers, Matrones and Maidens* (a translation of Bruto's *Young Gentlewoman*), for example, Salter recommends instead of books and the pen for writing, the 'Distaffe, and Spindle, Nedle and Thimble.'[45] But while these theorists were busy arguing whether and how women should be educated, a considerable portion of the female population was apparently reading. The number of books addressed to women by the turn of the century is the strongest though not the only evidence of that.[46]

Furthermore, developments in the printing press could combine with other factors to produce an effect much more advantageous to women than the various theories propounded. The educational revolution claimed by Stone and others[47] did not affect women as it affected men. The many educational establishments that were built in the late Tudor and early Stuart periods, mainly with endowments from wealthy merchants, were schools for the sons of the bourgeoisie, the future men in the public service. They were a response to a demand for more literate personnel and a means of climbing the social ladder. They prepared men for vocations not usually open to women. But if the educational revolution did not affect women by sending them to secondary schools,[48] it did create a more literate environment for many of them. Access to books of fathers and brothers could be beneficial for those women who had more leisure time than before. For the rise of a wealthy merchant class created a separation between the public world of the man and the private one of the woman, but not all women were worse off for that. Additionally, if we take into account that a sizeable portion of the middle class aspired to imitate aristocratic trends, we would expect the wealthy merchants to teach their daughters at least reading and writing. (The aristocracy were already educating their daughters in the vernacular if not in the classical languages as the early humanists had recommended.)

Women's access to literacy and books is quite important, as reading is not just a mechanical skill. It is an opportunity to broaden one's horizons, for to read means not simply to receive facts and information but also to enrich the imagination with possibilities not offered in everyday humdrum life. And could anyone strictly control what people read? Conservative theoreticians branded amorous literature immoral and especially inappropriate for women, but the latter apparently went on reading such material despite the repeated prohibitions. Louis B. Wright informs us that in addition to religious books, women read a great deal of fictional literature (romances of all types, love stories, and amorous poems). Lyly and Greene in particular were considered women's authors.[49] Nor could theorists stop developments in the printing press. Indeed the growth of the press is one of the principal features of the sixteenth and seventeenth centuries. From about 1575 onward a great variety of books was becoming available to an increasingly greater reading public. Bibles, devotional treatises, prayer books, almanacs, jest books, songs, how-to books, marriage guides, philosophical treatises, factual and fictional accounts of voyages, sonnets, plays, translations of Ovid and Ariosto, and erotic books – all comprised a bookseller's stock.[50] Thus humanist ideas combine with a number of social and technological developments to produce an amorphous situation which some women could find exploitable.

Meanwhile, the court and a number of aristocratic families promote a slightly different version of feminine conduct from that discussed above. Rather than following the prescriptions of Vives and Markham, they look to more liberal, and more suitable, models set forth in continental courtesy books like Castiglione's *The Book of The Courtier* and Guazzo's *Civil Conversations* translated in 1561 and 1581 respectively. These books address the demands of a new 'polite' society, which requires of women much more than literacy skills and invites them to participate in the activities of men. The profession of the lady-in-waiting was being reshaped to suit the needs of a new court. Like the position of the courtier, that of the lady-in-waiting was part of the larger system of patronage, which was based on an exchange of favours. To be a lady-in-waiting was not simply to be employed by the queen in the practical sense. It was a sign of royal favour towards the family of the young woman. When Queen Elizabeth took into service Mary Sidney (later Herbert), she meant to give a token of her sympathy for the loss of another daughter by the Sidneys.

The function of the ladies-in-waiting was twofold: to enhance the status of the queen and princess they were to serve and also to provide a milieu for the more permanently positioned courtier.[51] They were to take part in conversations and contests, and to encourage men in their accomplishments. Their public function demanded of them to follow not the rules of silence and obedience but those of controlled speech and gesture. As Ann Jones discusses, the requirements for the court lady focused not on the woman's capacity to hold her tongue but on her ability to manipulate speech effectively. Like the speech of the ordinary woman, that of the court lady was linked to sexuality. In *The Book of the Courtier*, Castiglione warns the lady of the many traps she has to avoid. She must be careful not to let people think that she would be sexually available. Such a reputation would jeopardize her standing in the queen's service and would considerably reduce her prospects for a successful marriage match. But unlike the ordinary wife, the court lady cannot remain silent. Her role as participant in polite conversation with men requires her to talk. Requirements for speech in this context conflict with those for sexual purity, but it is the lady's task to sort them out and to manoeuvre her way skilfully between the two. (Ann Jones aptly terms this a 'tightrope act.') She must assess what men might do or say and must pre-empt their responses if they are likely to place her in a disadvantageous position. But she must not assume a merely defensive stance either. She must learn to take up opportunities for self-display without giving the impression that she wants to attract attention. Gestures may be used, but effective speech is particularly important. The exercise of verbal skills, the ability to participate in public display – these, we might recall, are the qualities forbidden by Protestant theorists on feminine conduct. These are also the qualities useful in writing literature. By cultivating such qualities, courtly theory and practice formed an ideological contradiction to the dictum of feminine silence and enabled a small group of women to appear acceptably in public.

Of course the English court did not usually provide a venue for female literary activity. Elizabeth I, possibly the one English monarch who could have established a stable environment for such activity, was herself in an ideologically precarious position. Under attack from patriarchalists who assumed a male head in the commonwealth as well as in the home, she could not afford the political cost of a court prompting women to what were considered male pursuits. But even if England's court did not provide a milieu in which women could actually write, it did offer a kind of training ground for the acquisition of skills requisite for writing. Out of a half-dozen secular women authors and translators, three – Mary Herbert, Mary Wroth, and Aemilia Lanyer – were in court service at one time or another, as were also several of the influential patronesses of literature.

The principles of civil conduct, which collided with patri-archalist and Protestant ideologies, were not practised only at the royal court but also within many influential humanist households. The social system of fostering or 'placing out,' was very important in this respect. Placing children, especially daughters, in the service of a wealthier relative or acquaintance was a widely practised form of the larger system of patronage. Though it was a type of domestic service or apprenticeship, placing out was distinguished from ordinary servanthood by the existence of indentures, agreements of enrolment and release, obligations involved, service rendered, and other terms.[52] Theo-retically the system was based on the idea that parents were too fond of their children to discipline them properly. Practically, it achieved several other goals. As it applied primarily to young females, it provided a solution to the problem of formal training (carried out by the convents prior to the Reformation) and an opportunity to improve marriage prospects. For a young woman who left her parents' house when she was seven or eight, domestic service was a form of education and training in social conduct. She was supposed to receive instruction not only in house management but also in languages and music. Mistress Openwork in Middleton's *The Roaring Girl* provides an entertaining picture of the curriculum: 'he took me from my lady's service where I was well beloved of the steward; I had my Latin tongue and a spice of the French before I came to him' (Act II, Scene i). When the family that had received the charge were relatives, then the girl would be treated like the children of the people she served. This was the case, for example, with Margaret Clement, who, placed in the household of her uncle Sir Thomas More, received the same education as his daughters.

The system of fostering, however, did not produce only well-mannered ladies who could embroider, chat a little French, and play the lute. Placed in the urban households of prominent humanists, some women apparently turned domestic service into an opportunity to acquire high-level language skills. With sufficient encouragement from the host family and their useful acquaintances, they could then venture out into areas ordinarily closed to them. Sometimes domestic service was the only way for young women of the country to come to London, the centre of publishing and intellectual activity. Indeed the system of placing out seems to account for the presence of three secular writers from the middle ranks – Isabella Whitney, Margaret Tyler, and Aemilia Lanyer. All three of these women apparently acquired their academic training while in domestic service. Whitney presents herself as a servant out of a job; Margaret Tyler informs us that she had served in the family of Lord Howard, to whom she dedicates her translation of Ortuñez's romance; and Lanyer mentions that she had at some point been connected with the household of Lady Cumberland.

LITERARY ACTIVITY

In the preface to her translation of the Spanish romance *A Mirrour of Princely deedes and Knighthood* (1578), Margaret Tyler defends her act of translating a secular piece of literature and pleads with the reader thus: 'amongst my il willers, some I hope are not so straight that they would enforce me necessarily either not to write or to write of divinitie' (sig. A4).[53] In this passage, as well as in the rest of the preface, Tyler voices the most serious of the limitations pertaining to female writers in sixteenth-century England. The acceptable literary areas for women were basically two: religion and domesticity. Religion was a woman's prerogative which did not jeopardize her chastity (the graveness of the subject guaranteed sexual modesty), while the domestic scene (anything pertaining to children and the house) was her granted dominion. Translation was also an acceptable area for women to work in. Yet the permission to translate did not also carry with it a licence to cross the boundaries of gender and subject matter. Tyler's stout defence of her right to translate a love story is evidence of that, as is also the fact that most translations by women of that period are within the area of religion.

As may already be apparent, women's appearance in print and the attached permissions and prohibitions were closely linked to Renaissance notions regarding sexuality, authorship, and female inferiority. Publication was directly linked to aggressive sexuality: to appear in print was to appear in public and hence also to seek male attention. A woman who published exposed herself mentally to the public eye. Furthermore, since a woman was considered man's inferior in intellectual capacity, she could be accused of presumption or simply be denied agency of her work. Rachel Speght tells us that her *Melastomus* (1617) was attributed to her father and she writes her *Mortalities Memorandum* (1621) 'to prove them further futurely who have formerly deprived me of my due.'[54] Still, if she stayed within accepted subject parameters and acknowledged at least typologically her own inferiority (the apology for writing 'though a woman' was often included in dedications and prefaces), the sixteenth-century literary woman was relatively free from censure. But to write within the field of imaginative literature was most transgressive, for authorship of literature was considered a distinctly male activity. The female writer in the Renaissance, as well as in later times, had to struggle with the idea prevalent in patriarchal western culture that 'the text's author is a father, a procreator, an aesthetic patriarch.'[55] According to this idea, creative energy in a woman is anomalous and freakish. Hence as a male characteristic, authorship is 'essentially unfeminine.'[56] When Edward Denny, an aristocrat who recognized himself as the object of satire in *The Countess of Montgomeries Urania*, quarrelled with the author, Mary Wroth, he accused her of being a 'hermaphrodite' and told her to stay away from penning 'lascivious stories' and 'amorous toys'; he recommended instead that she follow the example of her aunt, the Countess of Pembroke, who translated 'holy books,' like the Psalms of David.[57] The restrictions and the general hostility towards women's literary endeavours sometimes led to the suppression of their work. This was the case with Wroth's *The Countess of Montgomeries Urania* (1621) and Cary's *The Tragedie of Mariam* (1613). The particular circumstances of the suppression of these two publications are discussed in the appropriate chapters, but generally when a controversy broke out, either in public or private circles, a woman had less chance of surviving it than did a man. (The cases I refer to concern public material; we do not know how much of women's literary work was suppressed in manuscript form.)

There were still other obstacles. The absence of appropriate female models was one of the most important. Especially in a society which considers female authorship transgressive, a woman writer needs models 'to legitimate her own rebellious endeavors.'[58] She needs it as assurance to herself and to others that she can produce art without fearing that her product might be categorized as second rate and she herself as whore, spinster, or anomalous creature.[59] The need for suitable models, rather than for any models, and the problem of access to them, is evident from the fact that women writers usually cite female precedents from the classics and the Bible. Debborah, Judith, Hester, Pallas, Cynthia, and the Muses are figures frequently mentioned. This shows how a woman's search for models was necessarily bound up with the defensive stance in which she was placed as a result of sexual suspicions. Lanyer's prefatory and dedicatory material in *Salve Deus Rex Judaeorum* (1611) resounds with names which carry a suggestion of intellectual capacity and sexual purity (Pallas, Cynthia, Debborah). Such names also appear in the controversy over the nature of women, the so-called *querrelle de femmes*.[60] However useful, such mythological figures could not fill the need for alliance with female writers closer in time to the sixteenth century. Did Englishwomen of the Renaissance have access to works of their more immediate predecessors in England and on the continent? Were they acquainted with the lives and works of medieval poets and mystics like Julian of Norwich, Marie de France and Christine de Pizan? We do not know, but such names do not appear in the literary publications of Renaissance Englishwomen. Some of these authors were not available in print; others, like St Catherine, who is said to have defeated fifty philosophers in theological argument, were probably suppressed by the Reformation; still others like Marie de France and the female trobaritz, if known, would not have been appropriate as authority figures in an effort to avoid the connection of literature with sexuality. Precedents closer to home were actually in the process of being established, and women writers of the late Renaissance apparently built on the works of their immediate predecessors. Thus Elizabeth Cary writes in a dramatic mode already made known through the publication of Mary Herbert's translation of *Antonie* (1595); Lanyer benefits from the tradition of women as writers of religious works and feminist pamphlets, as well as from the practice of women as patrons of literature; and Wroth experiments with the poetic structures of her aunt and uncle.

Renaissance notions about female sexuality and intellectual inferiority are linked to the absence of a suitable language as well as to the search for models. In the patriarchal establishment of the early modern period (and arguably of later periods), the language of women was essentially the language of men and as such it incorporated a misogynist bias. In Mary Wroth's *Urania*, one of the characters admonishes her female friend thus: 'Shall your excellent virtues be drowned in the Sea of weaknesse? . . . you that have been admired for a Masculine spirit, will you descend below the poorest Feminine in love?' (1621 edition, p. 398). The use of such language necessarily circumscribed and often contradicted women writers' attempts to escape stereotypes and establish new meanings. Furthermore, since men dominated the printed page, the terms in which women could criticize dominant gender ideology were men's terms, and these offered very little basis for substantial criticism. Male debates on the man–woman relationship almost always revolved around issues of morality: women were either good or bad. There was no established discourse on sexual difference in socio-economic terms. This inevitably limited what women could say about their relative position in society.

The lack of an accessible venue for a collective mixed-group literary activity was also a barrier to Englishwomen who wished to write. Ann Jones's recent comparative study, *The Currency of Eros: Women's Love Lyric in Europe, 1540–1620*,[61] makes us aware of the similarities in ideologies of femininity across European borders, but it also alerts us to important differences at the level of actual practice. In sixteenth-century Lyon, Poitiers, and Paris, female literary salons provided an active context for competition and literary improvisation. In Protestant England things were less favourable. Though the court and the urban humanist households offered an opportunity for public appearance and for the exercise of verbal skills necessary for writing, they did not actually provide a substitute for a salon like that of Madeleine and Catherine Des Roches. The Pembroke household at Wilton became the centre of literary activity for at least one woman, the countess of the estate itself, but it included mainly male participants.[62]

Englishwomen responded in various ways to the obstacles they encountered. But they often took an indirect course. Translation became a popular form of literary expression among women of the period, especially in the acceptable subject of religion. This is not surprising. Though in the Renaissance translation was much more highly ranked than it has been since, it was still a less active and hence less masculine literary activity than original composition. It called for a relatively passive role.

A woman translator could thus hide behind another author (usually male) and protect herself against accusations pertaining to ideas and content. 'The invention, disposition, trimming, and what els in this story, is wholy an other mans, my part none therein but the translation,' says Margaret Tyler in the preface to her *Mirrour*. This indirect and essentially defensive use of translation becomes more evident when we consider the nature of the translations. As Mary Ellen Lamb remarks, the 'translations of Renaissance women are different from the translations of Renaissance men in being exceedingly literal.'[63] The utilization of permitted areas, especially of religion, became an indirect way of self-assertion in literary expression. Writing religious *and* secular works became a way of justifying both. The respectable name that is acquired from the versification of the *Psalms* can also legitimate the translation of a play like *Antonie*. A woman who has earned respectability through her devotion to religious matters can also translate or write secular works without much risk. (Religion can also be used to justify other intellectual exercises, like the study of foreign languages. Mary Ellen Lamb mentions the example of Anne Cooke Bacon who explicitly appeals to the religious nature of her translation to justify the study of Italian.)[64] The permitted areas of religion can further be used as a strategy for approaching secular issues. Lanyer in *Salve Deus* sings the praises of Christ but also engages in a feminist defence of Eve.

Voicing the modesty topos was another indirect way of self-assertion in the literary field. Most women, though not all, include in the dedication or preface of their work an apology which recognizes, at least for the sake of appearance, the inferiority of the work on account of the author's sex. Dedicating a work to a man or to a respectable woman, likewise provided an indirect strategy for venturing into publication. Both Tyler and Lanyer dedicate their works to respectable and aristocratic former employers. Some women present themselves as reluctant to publish what they have written and cite the persuasive influence of friends or acquaintances. This is the case with Whitney and Tyler. Others, like the young Elizabeth Cary, keep much of what they write in private circulation, until someone with greater authority prompts them to publish their work. In this respect, women usually relied on support from men sympathetic to their accomplishments, and there were a

21

few such men around. For we must remember that it was not only the Lord Dennys who carried influence but also humanists like Sir John Davies. The latter praised women authors and even admonished them for publishing too little of what they wrote. 'You press the Press with little you have made,' says Davies, addressing himself to Lady Falkland, Lady Pembroke, and Lady Redford in the dedication of the *The Muses Sacrifice or Divine Meditations*.[65] (Perhaps it is not coincidental that Cary's *Mariam* appeared in print in 1613, a year after Davies's exhortation.)

Patronage, especially self-interested patronage like that of Mary Herbert, was sometimes an indirect strategy of self-expression and channelling of creative energy. The large number of books dedicated to women shows that the latter responded actively and favourably to authors; otherwise, as Hull remarks, they would not have been sought out.[66] Aristocratic patronesses were an exploitable group for male authors, but what apparently made them exploitable was the fact that patronage addressed particular female needs and sensitivities. If we consider that to patronize a work is to be in some sense the father of that work, the one who makes authorship possible (patron= father), a woman who serves as patron also indirectly channels her own creative energies, especially when she commissions the works she patronizes.

A very small number of women (Wroth, Tyler, and the authors of feminist pamphlets) use direct challenge as their strategy for writing. Without apologies and without many diplomatic circumventions, these women claim their right to enter the literary field. As the analysis of the texts reveals, strategies for acquiring a voice inextricably combine with strategies for other purposes in writing. Women writers who wish to be profitably heard must acquire credibility. This means that they must accommodate rather than reject dominant notions regarding virtuous female behaviour. Voicing opposition to a certain oppressive idea must be done by underpinning other conventional ideas. Furthermore, a woman writer in a patriarchal culture must develop strategies against her own internalization of the oppressive ideologies around her; for when she experiences conflict between her desire and what she has been taught is right and proper, she must try to accommodate both desire and the ideology that denies it. Such strategies – whether consciously or unconsciously used

– profoundly determine the shape of women's literary style. I use the term style in its broad sense to denote the way ideas are expressed or handled by an author. What is included in the text and what is left out, the manner in which ideas are developed and contradictions or tensions resolved, the techniques employed in the text to render particular characters sympathetic or situations workable, these are all matters of style. Furthermore, when I use terms like negotiation or appropriation to refer to certain processes or strategies, I do not mean to imply that the author is necessarily conscious of employing these.

The strategies I have just referred to are not peculiar to women, nor are the types of ideologies women oppose. In a period when writers depended to a a large extent on patronage, when censorship on political and religious grounds was heavily imposed, and when to publish for profit was considered somewhat demeaning, male writers often developed and deployed similar strategies. But when used by female writers, such strategies acquire a different meaning because they are responses to an ideology and culture that denied women self-expression.[67] Similarly, voicing opposition to dominant ideology is potentially more subversive in the case of a woman, because of the different position of the two sexes in Renaissance society. As Jonathan Dollimore points out, subversiveness depends on 'the context of its articulation: to whom, how many and in what circumstances.'[68] Thus Philip Sidney's criticism of his culture in his romance is less transgressive than Mary Wroth's in hers, not only because the *Urania* is a more oppositional work than the *Arcadia* in matters of gender, but primarily because the female author is not supposed to be writing romances in the first place. Also, a woman publishing a play about Cleopatra is not the same as a man doing it. The point is not, therefore, that women's writing is different from men's, but that it has to be *read* differently.

THE TEXTS AND THE APPROACH

In my choice of authors and texts I have not aimed to be exhaustive. My focus has been on those women who wrote or translated and published secular literary works and who raised an oppositional voice. I have accordingly chosen for close study six writers and translators – Isabella Whitney, Margaret

Tyler, Mary Herbert, Elizabeth Cary, Aemilia Lanyer, and Mary Wroth. These are women who published a considerable volume of secular literature, though some of them wrote or translated religious works as well. Chronologically, they fall roughly within the second half of the English Renaissance (1565–1640), but that is because women who published in the first half of the period dealt almost exclusively with religious subjects. In my group of authors I have not included the two queens of the period (Elizabeth Tudor and Mary Stuart) because they do not seem to me to be typical of other women at that point of English culture, and also because they have already received adequate critical attention. Nor have I included women of English origin brought up on the continent.

My purpose in analysing the works of these women is manifold. My principal purpose is to determine their opposition to contemporary dominant ideologies, especially those on gender. How far do these women contest such ideologies and what do they aim for? Text analysis shows that they are limited in the extent to which they can carry their contestation and in the alternatives they can propose. The limitations are largely discursive. The unavailability of appropriate language and critical discourse creates an impasse. But other factors, such as the author's purpose in writing, her social class, and her financial position, also play a role. How do these factors and the various cultural restrictions determine what the female writers finally say? In the process of answering these questions I consider important related issues, such as strategies of assertion and feminine awareness. Since these women write in a culture which inhibits their intellectual activity, especially as regards the writing of literature, they must employ strategies that will help them acquire a literary voice (i.e. that will enable them to enter the literary field). How do these strategies interconnect with those used for other purposes, like writing for profit or voicing criticism? In my discussion of their opposition to contemporary ideology, I have used Raymond Williams's useful distinction between the 'dominant' (the values and ideas currently in effect), the 'residual' (those formed in the past but still practised in the present), and the 'emergent' (new values, meanings, and relationships).[69]

In determining women's oppositional voices, I have taken care not to force the texts into any particular pattern nor to ignore those parts which conflict with the oppositional voice. For the tensions, contradictions, and divergences in the texts reveal how these women tried to reconcile (or not to reconcile) the values they internalized and those they contested. In this I have regarded the texts not as reflections of any given reality, or spontaneous authorial expressions, but as places where various meanings are constructed and negotiated.

I have come to the texts with the types of questions raised by much recent work in cultural materialist and feminist criticism. But I have also used certain 'traditional' concepts like intentionality and authorial psychology. Though contentious, such concepts need, I believe, to be re-examined.

Within literary criticism, intentionality has hitherto been viewed mainly in relation to the text's ontology – its relative autonomy or dependence. First New Criticism attacked intentionality as a factor 'external' to an autonomous, all-containing literary text. Structuralism later discredited it from an opposite direction: the reader, rather than the author, was to have the final word on the construction of meaning. Within feminist criticism there has been a tendency to claim for the female literary writer an intention to solve problems of gender. Materialist feminist critics have rightly censured this tendency. Michele Barrett, for example, contends that 'to construe a novelist as a sociologist manqué' is to ignore the fictional character of literature and to imply an unsatisfactory 'identification of text and female author.'[70] Barrett is correct, but even in her critique there is a general uneasiness about the subject of intention, which is eschewed rather than explored. The subtle but crucial problems inherent in the process of composition remain unresolved.

There is indeed a great difference between presenting the author as a directive agent in the text on the one hand, and exploring her awareness and handling of oppressive notions in her culture on the other. This kind of distinction has not been dealt with in recent feminist criticism; yet it is an important one, especially when we speak about women writing in a hostile environment. If we cannot speak of a 'sociologist manqué,' surely we can speak of a woman writer's awareness of prohibitions and her conscious attempts to challenge or deal with these. If, for example, a woman's literary work has been subjected to criticism, is it not valid to speak of her attempt to

25

use certain strategies so as to prevent or pre-empt criticism in her next work? Is it not relevant to point out signs of her conscious effort to circumvent particular prohibitive notions?

There seems to be a very thin line between an author's intention and an author's awareness of her position in relation to the ideology of her culture. Authorial awareness, intention, and psychology seem at times difficult to extricate, as psychology and the process of writing are closely related. In any given context, a writer may be said to have the reader looking over his/her shoulder. Thus Virginia Woolf may metaphorically and literally speak about the 'Angel in the House' as an obstacle to women's writing. Pressure or anxiety about social obstacles can work at the psychological level at the time of composition, and this may manifest itself in the style. For example, the sense of being a female doing something transgressive may affect what a woman will write and what she will stop short of. This account of agency and composition is compatible with the concept of texts as places of negotiation and contestation of meaning.

Also, to speak about a woman author's personal skills (e.g., ingenuity and critical discernment) is not to underestimate the effect of discursive formations on her writing. On the contrary, it is precisely because these formations were very strong that great personal skill was required to counter them. What has just been discussed is a methodological problem fundamental to feminist studies. My concern has not been to solve the problem as such. Working from the texts outwards, I have tried to do justice to the questions that arose in the process of textual analysis.

In the chapters that follow I have grouped the authors according to class, chronology, and major concern. Grouping by genre was an alternative option, since the literary medium women chose (particularly in the case of closet drama and romance) often suggested the direction of expression. But an arrangement by class, subject matter, and chronological context appeared even more suggestive because it revealed differences as well as similarities due to those factors. Finally, in my discussions of these authors I have taken into account the fact that they are still relatively unknown, and so I have tried to provide as much relevant information as possible.

2

SERVANT GIRLS
CLAIMING MALE DOMAIN

In the middle decades of the sixteenth century prospects for women were not good. Education was available only to a small percentage of women, mainly in the upper classes, while theoretical discourse was generally negative in its attitude towards female literary activity. Though official opinion was divided over the amount and kind of learning that should be allowed to women of various classes, all agreed that women should not take up writing poems, plays, and romances, or, worse yet, publish them. Women of authorial ambition had to confine themselves to religious and domestic subjects. It is no mere coincidence that until the late 1560s no Englishwoman had published any significant volume of secular literature, at least according to existing records.

In this generally unfavourable climate, Isabella Whitney and Margaret Tyler seem to have broken ground, the first by publishing two volumes of poetry between 1567 and 1573 and the second by translating and publishing a Spanish romance in 1578. The two women share several characteristics. They are both early secular writers of middle-class background, self-educated, and ex-servants at the time they write. These similarities suggest already that Whitney and Tyler turned certain cultural obstacles into opportunities for intellectual development. Service in aristocratic households, for example, became an opportunity for learning.

Apparently profiting from the libraries of their humanist employers, both women managed to acquire a broad education that included vernacular as well as classical sources. At the same time, non-aristocratic status probably offered a relative degree of freedom.[1] Unlike an aristocratic woman, an ex-servant girl like Whitney had more to gain than to lose from venturing into socially disapproved territory. Coming to the capital, working as domestic servant, and then becoming a writer was not the typical route of a servant girl, or of any girl in the sixteenth century, but typical or not, it was evidently possible.

ISABELLA WHITNEY: WARNING WOMEN TO BEWARE OF MEN

Whitney apparently came to London from Cheshire, took up service in a family, and at the loss of this position turned to writing.[2] She produced two volumes of poetry: *The Copy of a Letter . . . With an Admonition* (c. 1567) and *A Sweet Nosegay* (1573). The first contains an abandoned mistress's lament in the Ovidian mode as well as a warning to young women to beware of men's deceptive behaviour; the second volume includes moral adages, epistles to various persons familiar to the author, and a description of commercial London ('The Wyll and Testament of Isabella Whitney').[3] Popular in tone, the two volumes focus on interpersonal relationships, especially those between men and women. At times daring in her criticism of men and at other times laid back, Whitney exploits the ideology she inherits in order to make herself heard. Her work shows how a sixteenth-century woman manages to speak creditably in print and how a complex group of factors revolving around gender interconnect and finally shape her work. It thus reveals much about the interrelation of gender and style and the negotiating processes at work in the text.

Whitney sometimes displays what Betty Travitsky calls a 'carefree' spirit.[4] This is especially apparent in 'The Wyll and Testament,' where the author describes with humour and nonchalance her apparently familiar city of London. And it may be seen also in her first volume of poetry. However, Whitney's ease and self-confidence sometimes belie an underlying anxiety related to cultural restrictions. The customary apology which attributes the imperfections of a work to the sex of its author is usually one indication of the constraints felt by women writers. Whitney does not exactly ask forgiveness, as most other women writers of this period do, but her work contains subtler forms of apology which are expressed without any particular attention drawn to them. Perhaps the most interesting apology is the one

implied in the opening lines of *A Sweet Nosegay, or pleasant Posye*
where she addresses the reader:

> This harvest tyme, I harvestlesse,
>   and servicelesse also:
> And subject unto sicknesse, that
>   abroade I could not go.
> Had leasure good, (though learning lackt)
>   some study to apply:
> To reade such Bookes, wherby I thought
>   my selfe to edifye.
> Sometimes the Scriptures I perusd,
>   but wantyng a Devine:
> For to resolve mee in such doubts,
>   as past this head of mine
> To understand: I layd them by.

(A5v)[5]

Anticipating charges for occupying her time improperly,
Whitney here apologizes indirectly first for spending her time
reading and then for not reading religious books. Her culture
generally viewed women's learning with suspicion; any time
devoted to reading was justified only in so far as it was spent
on the scriptures. Furthermore, post-Reformation patriarchy
stipulated that a woman must have a divine to guide her in
her interpretations. Whitney's self-depiction as a 'serviceless'
woman sick in bed shows her skill in deploying cultural
stipulations advantageously (a divine is not something one
can have at an arm's reach); but it also indicates that a woman's
preoccupation with secular books called for justification.

Whitney's repeated apologies for borrowing Plat's material[6]
and her praises of his work also suggest fear of accusation. In
the prefatory material of *A Sweet Nosegay* and her 'Farewell
to the Reader,' Whitney speaks about using the 'flowers' of
'anothers growing,' of being 'bolde to come when as I wyll
. . . and to chuse of all his flowers, which may my fancy fill'
(A4v, B3r). She conscientiously refers the reader to 'Master
Plat his ground.' This attempt to protect herself from being
accused of literary stealing reveals how susceptible to criticism
a woman's work was. In an age when male writers lifted
material wholesale from classical and contemporary sources
without even troubling about acknowledgements, Whitney's

excessive concern seems to suggest that the liberties taken by men could not automatically also be taken by women writers.

These apologies are expressed in defensive terms, as women writers' apologies usually are. But offence can also be a form of defence, and Whitney occasionally becomes offensive in order to control response and pre-empt criticism. Early in the *Nosegay* volume, for example, she spikes the guns of her readers by placing conditions on the attitude with which they are to approach her work:

> But yf thy mind infected be,
>   then these wyll not prevayle.
>   (A7r)

> I must request you spoyle them not,
>   nor doo in peeces teare them:
> But if thy selfe doo lothe the sent
>   geve others leave to weare them.
>   (C5v)

By means of these permissions and prohibitions, Whitney manages to place the reader rather than herself on the defensive and to shift the focus to terms more advantageous for her.

There are additional reasons why Whitney's ease cannot be taken as lack of anxiety altogether. 'Certain familier Epistles' in the *Nosegay* collection register the author's long depression, the cause of which seems to have been gossip against her. In 'Is. W. to C.B.' she tells her friend 'how some me spite,' and in answering, C.B. reassures her thus:

> Yf eveil words and other wants,
>   have brought thee to this woe:
> Remember how that Christ him selfe,
>   on earth was even so:
> Thy friends that have thee knowne of long,
> Will not regard thy enemies tong.
>   (D7r)

Because she never clearly describes the 'eveil words' or the 'enemies,' our attempts to locate the precise problem are frustrated. But though we cannot speculate with any certainty, we can at least pose the possibility that the 'eveil words' of the enemies might have something to do with her being a woman and a writer. Two clues lend support to this conjecture. In answering her plea for help, C.B. defends her virtue and her character, implying that they have been under attack:

> The vertue that hath ever beene,
>   within thy tender brest:
> Which I from yeare to yeare, have seene,
>   in all thy deedes exprest:
> Doth me persueade thy enemies lye,
> And in that quarell would I dye.
>
> (D7r)

Also, the sickness she complains of in 'The Auctor to the Reader' is apparently mental depression connected with her writing. It seems to vanish as soon as she comes upon Plat's book (A6r) which is the source of her A Sweet Nosegay. However we interpret these passages, one thing becomes apparent: Whitney has not escaped the restrictions of her culture.

Economic and other constraints

As a middle-class, self-supporting woman writing in the sixteenth century, Whitney is subject to several constraints, which ultimately determine the content and style of her work. The first, most obvious one, is the economic.

At various places in her work Whitney refers to her adverse financial position. In the passage quoted above from the opening address to the reader in A Sweet Nosegay, she speaks about being 'harvestlesse and servicelesse' (A5v), and in the epistle 'To her Sister Misteris A.B.' she says that the lack of 'household cares' has made her turn to writing (D2r). If these references describe her financial condition, it does indeed look as though she was in financial straits. Apparently she thought to alleviate this condition by publishing. Her dealing mainly with popular material and her attempts to reach a wide readership further suggest economic motives for writing.

In The Professional Writer in Elizabethan England, Miller informs us that 'by the end of the sixteenth century the custom of paying authors (including many of the amateurs) for manuscripts had been firmly established.'[7] Although the fees paid to authors were usually inadequate to provide a solution to a life-long economic problem, they were enough to relieve an author from a temporary financial strait. Much bargaining and negotiation went on between publishers, printers, and authors, and often the latter responded to a publisher's specifications regarding marketable material. Although not all printers were money-grabbing, profit guided most of what they put out.

Whitney seems aware of literary trends and of popular taste. It is quite likely that she worked in close communication with Richard Jones, the publisher of both her works and also of two other poetical miscellanies to which Whitney might have contributed anonymously.[8] (Jones apparently specialized in popular material, mainly ballads and broadsides, but also printed many practical books on various non-literary subjects.) It is thus probable that Whitney received some compensation from her publisher.

Unlike her male contemporaries, Whitney could not use the system of literary patronage. As a woman writer, especially a secular one, she had very remote chance, if any, of finding a patron who would support her. She wasn't supposed to be writing in the first place. Whitney none the less seems to be making an attempt to solicit patronage by dedicating her work to George Mainwaring, a close friend of her family and one whom she apparently knew from childhood. (She refers to him as 'chiefe' among her friends.) She was therefore acquainted with his attitude and ran little risk of offending him. At first the dedication appears to be a gift of appreciation for past favours, but then, with a conventional manoeuvre, she asks for his protection of her work and promises to produce 'a more dayntier thing' in the future (A5r). One wonders how much support, if any, a dedication of this sort brought her. It is quite likely that the intangible benefits from having the name of a prominent man on her work and from his protection were more useful to her as a woman writer.

Another constraint has to do with social survival. Isabella Whitney had to be diplomatic in her writing if she did not wish to be considered a rebel or an oddity and to alienate herself completely from her social environment. Her excessive preoccupation with 'foes' and the circulating gossip she alludes to in 'Certain familier Epistles' already indicate difficulties in social relations.

A third major constraint is the language available to her for expression. Without any precedents for her to follow, her ideas could only be expressed in terms generated by male writers – true and false, virtuous and wanton, good and bad. Even worse, the linguistic structure and idiom were already gendered at the expense of the female sex and hence a handicap to a woman writer. A simple example which offers only a glimpse into this complex problem comes from Whitney's *Admonition* in *The Copy of a Letter*:

> Beware of fair and painted talk,
>   beware of flattery tongues,
> The Mermaides do pretend no good
>   for all their pleasant Songs.
>
>   (A6r)

The tension and contradiction in this metaphor show how difficult and self-undermining it was for a woman to contest meanings with a language that was pointed against her.

The Copy of a Letter

The Copy of a Letter . . . to her unconstant Lover. With an Admonition to al yong Gentilwomen (volume undated but having an entry date of 1566–7 in the Stationer's Register) is the first published attack on men by an Englishwoman. Written in the form of the traditional and popular lament poem, it also shares the spirit of later feminist pamphlets, like those of Jane Anger.[9] On the whole, the two pieces in *The Letter* volume constitute Whitney's strongest criticism of conventional gender ideology. Especially in *The Admonition*, she reverses several cultural assumptions and provides a counter-picture of the male/female relationship. The means of expressing the criticism is once more particularly interesting, for it reveals the obstacles involved and the skill required to work around them. Criticism of dominant gender ideology is not expressed by inventing a new language or setting up new sets of values for the behaviour of the two sexes but by exploiting the conventions of the poem's genre[10] and deploying dominant notions. As Ann Jones points out, throughout *The Letter* and *The Admonition* Whitney echoes

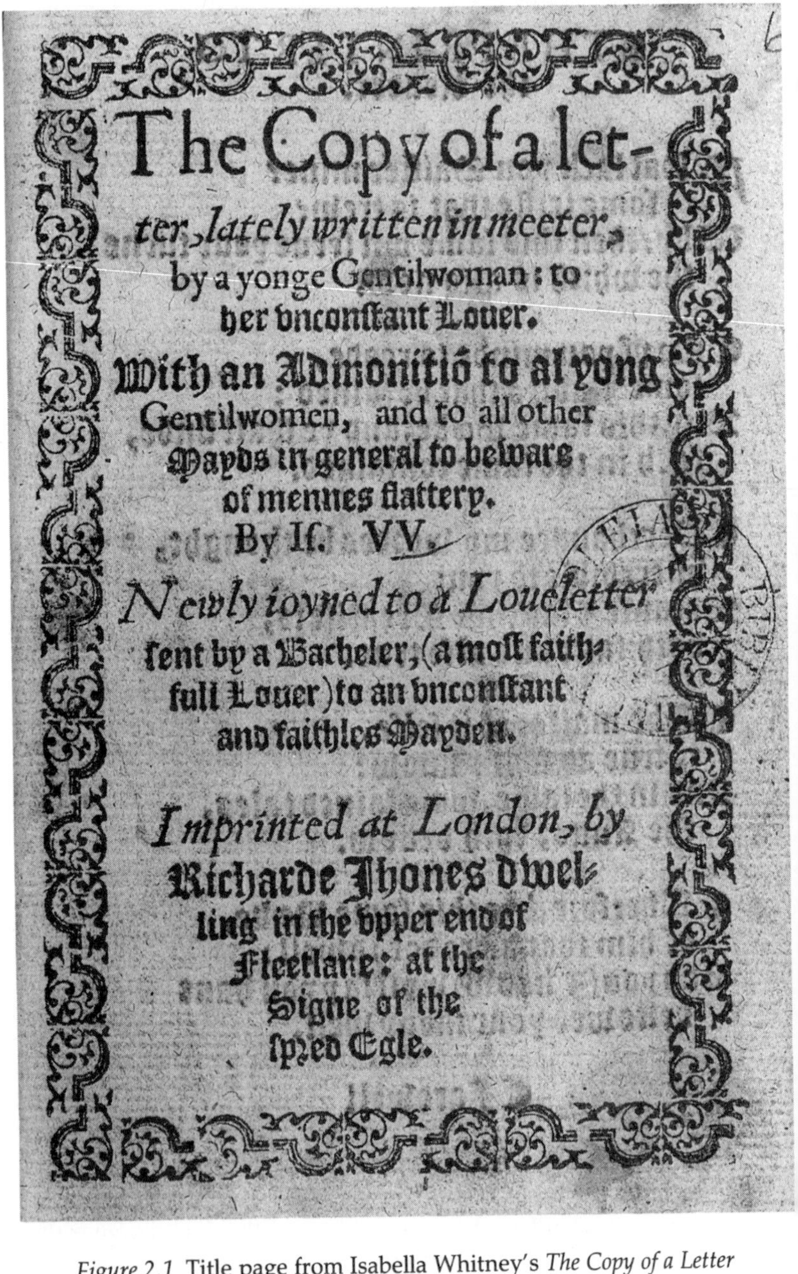

The Copy of a let-

ter, *lately written in meeter,*
by a yonge Gentilwoman : to
her vnconstant Louer.

With an Admonitió to al yong
Gentilwomen, and to all other
Mayds in general to beware
of mennes flattery.
By Is. VV.

Newly ioyned to a Loueletter
sent by a Bacheler, (a most faithfull Louer) to an vnconstant
and faithles Mayden.

Imprinted at London, by
Richarde Jhones dwel-
ling in the vpper end of
Fleetlane: at the
Signe of the
spred Egle.

Figure 2.1 Title page from Isabella Whitney's *The Copy of a Letter*
(London: Richard Jhones, 1567).

conduct-book commonplaces on feminine virtues and proper feminine behaviour.[11] Such a strategy permits her to escape the Ovidian victim/loquacious whore double bind. It also makes it possible for her to establish a respectable speaking voice and hence to attract a wider reading public.

In *The Copy of a Letter* Whitney speaks from several perspectives, shifting her critical position from rejected mistress to marriage counsellor and to representative of her sex. This polyphonic persona enables her among other things to elude classification as a type.

As a rejected mistress (and victim) she repeats her dissatisfaction with her lover's inconstancy, but does so in a way which shows awareness of the emotive overreaction traditionally associated with women in general and the Ovidian tragic heroines in particular. There is no screaming, no tearing of hair, no anger here:

> But if I cannot please your minde,
>   for wants that rest in me:
> Wed whom you list, I am content,
>   your refuse for to be.
>
> It shall suffice me simple soule,
>   of thee to be forsaken:
> And it may chance although not yet
>   you wish you had me taken.
>
>   (A4r)

Whitney victimizes herself not through loud lamentations or exaggerated descriptions of her love but through a quiet acceptance of her lover's rejection and break of promises. Earlier, in the second quatrain of the poem, she even offers friendship to him: 'You know I alwayes wisht you wel.' This representation of a composed female reaction is a refutation of both the Ovidian mode and the blackmailing threats of the lover of the sonnet.

From the position of the marriage counsellor, a role that in her culture had belonged only to men writers, she advises her lover on the virtues of his future wife:

> For she that shal so happy be,
>   of thee to be elect:
> I wish her vertues to be such,
>   she nede not be suspect.

I rather wish her HELENS face,
   then one of HELENS trade:
With chastnes of PENELOPE
   the which did never fade.

A LUCRES for her constancy,
   and THISBIE for her trueth.
               (A4r–A4v)

These requirements are not much different from those advocated in contemporary conduct books and sermons. But as Ann Jones correctly remarks, the citation of such requirements actually allows her to invert the power relation between herself and her unfaithful lover and so to land in a more advantageous position.[12] From this position Whitney catches her lover and hence also the men of her culture in an ideological contradiction: they set up the rules of marriage by prescribing the ideal virtues they look for in a wife, but they finally refuse to play the game fairly. Having just listed these required virtues, Whitney says:

Perchance, ye will think this thing, rare
   in on[e] woman to fynd:
Save Helens beauty, al the rest
   the Gods have me assignd.
               (A4v)

The implied question is, What else do you want? Traditionally it was women who were supposed to desire marriage and to set traps to catch husbands, and it was men who were supposed to seek freedom. But Whitney uses no traps, while her fiancé is leaving her only to marry somewhere else: 'But sith you shal a Husband be/ God send you a good wyfe' (A2r). She in fact implies in the passage quoted below that a single life is not a bad state; her main point is that if he wants to marry, he might as well marry her since he promised to do so:

And if you cannot be content
   to lead a single lyfe?
(Although the same right quiet be)
   then take me to your wife.
               (A2v)

From the standpoint of a woman who represents her sex, Whitney criticizes men's deceptive practices and their equally deceptive self-representation in literature and history. With her limited informal education, Whitney surveys historical and mythological sources in order to show a cross-section of gender attributes as they have been constructed by western culture. She cites examples from a well-known list of classical heroes (Theseus, Aeneas, Jason, Paris), while she shows that their heroic reputation has actually rested on the shameful exploitation of women:

> For they, for their unfaithfulnes,
>   did get perpetuall fame:
> Fame? wherefore dyd I terme it so?
>   I should have cald it shame.
>
> (A3v)

Exposing male practices as deceptive and predatory is also the target in *The admonition by the Auctor, to all yong Gentilwomen: And to al other Maids being in Love*, Whitney's strongest attack on men. The author begins her advice to young members of her sex by reversing certain conventional assumptions regarding male/female behaviour:

> Beware of fayre and painted talke,
>   beware of flattering tonges.
>
> (A6r)

That is, she transfers onto men the deceptive qualities traditionally attributed to women. And rather than quoting Ovid as an authority for proving the truth of male claims, she cites him in order to disclose the history of the discourse that teaches men how to be deceptive:

> Some use the teares of Crocodiles,
>   contrary to their hart:
> And yf they cannot alwayes weep,
>   they wet their Cheekes by Art.
>
> Ovid, within his Art of love,
>   doth teach them this same knacke
> to wet their hand and touch their eies:
>   so oft as teares they lacke.
>
> (A6r)

It is this kind of institutionalized deception, Whitney argues, that women have to be educated (warned) to detect:

> Or if Demophoons deceite,
>   to Phillis had ben tolde:
> She had not ben transformed so,
>   as Poets tell of olde.
>   (A7r)

A distinctly feminist attitude in *The Admonition*, one that sets Whitney further apart from the conduct-book writers she strategically echoes, is her attempt to establish solidarity with her female readers as members of the same sex. This is quite clear when she addresses men directly, thus placing them on the opposite side of the fence. The language used reveals a great deal:

> And wyll *ye* not leave of? but still
>   delude *us* in this wise?
> Sith it is so, *we* trust *we* shall,
>   take hede to fained lies.
>   (A6r; emphasis added)

Used by a woman, this type of language suggests more than an argument about deception. The *we/ye* opposition signifies an identification with other women. This is the closest Whitney comes to expressing a feminist consciousness: seeing women as an oppressed and persecuted group and siding with them. Whitney's final message in the poem, expressed in the same type of feminist language, may be seen as an attempt at consciousness raising:

> And since the fish that reason lacks
>   once warned doth beware:
> Why should not *we* take hede to that
>   that turneth us to care.
>   (A8v; emphasis added)

Betty Travitsky cites this passage as evidence that Whitney's advice is practical rather than rhetorical.[13] It is practical; and because the advice is addressed to women from the first person plural (*we*) point of view, it shares the potential effect of the feminist pamphlets.

A Sweet Nosegay

The tone is much lower in her second work. In *A Sweet Nosegay, Or pleasant Posye: contayning a hundred and ten Phylosophicall Flowers*, Whitney appears elusive, restrained, and even conventional. Occasionally, as in the following stanzas, she surprises us with her direct jibes at the supposedly wiser sex:

65

The lovers teres, wil soone appease
   his Ladyes angry moode:
But men will not be pacified,
   if wemen weep a flood.

(B9v)

76

Affection fond deceaves the wise
   and love maks men such noddyes
That to their selves they seeme as dead
   yet live in other boddies.

(C1v)

But such passages are rare. In the moral adages that she versifies, she does not substantially change the proverbial notions constitutive of contemporary dominant ideology. And even when she advises her two 'younger Sisters servinge in London,' her message is not basically different from that of middle-class conduct books on restrained feminine behaviour. Furthermore, Whitney refrains from boldly asserting her identity as a writer. In her epistle 'To her Sister Misteris A.B.' she speaks about it in qualifying terms:

Good Sister so I you commend,
   to him that made us all:
I know you huswyfery intend,
   though I to writing fall:
Therefore no lenger shall you stay,
From businesse, that profit may.

Had I a Husband, or a house,
   and all that longes therto

39

Myselfe could frame about to rouse,
  as other women doo:
But til some houshold cares mee tye,
My bookes and Pen I wyll apply.
                    (D2r)

Writing is here presented as a temporary job, something to do while waiting for a husband, a house, 'and all that longes therto.'

Why does Whitney appear more elusive, more restrained, and more conformist in the *Nosegay* collection? The answer has undoubtedly to do in part with the biased language she inherits and the genre she is writing in. But her attitude in this volume might also be linked to strategies for commercial success and for fending off criticism. What little evidence there is, mainly in her collection, suggests that economic and social constraints might have weighed more heavily in the production of this volume than in that of the previous one.

We know that Whitney's name had appeared in print as the author of *The Copy of a Letter* before the *Nosegay* and that Richard Jones had published both works. The first fact (previous appearance in print) could mean that pressure from cultural constraints was intensified by possible social criticism that *The Letter* might have provoked. Her obsession about people spoiling her 'flowers' – noticeably present in the verse epistles and the prefatory material of the *Nosegay* – seems symptomatic of the author's anxiety about the reception of her work. The word 'spite' appears frequently. In 'The Auctor to the Reader,' for instance, she warns off 'such greedy guts, as come with spite to toote.' This, combined with her reference to 'C.B.' and his defence of Whitney against the 'enemies tong,' hints at the idea that the *Nosegay* was composed under social scrutiny. Social criticism in this case, however, apparently did not preclude at least some commercial success, for it is unlikely that Richard Jones would have agreed to publish her second work, had the returns from *The Letter* been too bad. It seems more likely that author and printer saw the potential of the market. Indeed, there are clear indications that the *Nosegay* collection was produced with an eye to a wide reading public.

The *Nosegay* as a collection of assorted pieces seems to have been designed to reach several popular audiences. The main pieces which constitute the volume would have appealed to the average reader. The first major piece, which occupies about one-third of the entire book, consists of moral adages, or 'one hundred and ten philosophical flowers.' It seems to be the feature item; the volume begins with this part and also bears its name. The literature of the pseudo-Senecan *sententiae* was in great demand, and Whitney was apparently making an attempt to cash in on its popularity. Her 'philosophical flowers' are a popularized version of Plat's *Floures of Philosophie*, published a year earlier. Whitney elaborated and set in ballad meter Plat's short prose sentences which were an advantageous source for her. Although his style was academic, his subject was potentially popular and at the same time non-controversial. Hence Whitney could reap financial profits by popularizing it without running the risk of being criticized.

'Certain familier Epistles,' the second part of the *Nosegay*, is a series of verse letters to and from various friends and relatives of the author, including her two younger sisters serving in London. This part would have attracted female readers in general and the large female servant population of the capital in particular.[14] Although Whitney's epistles are not formalized enough to serve as writing models (as Richardson's were in the eighteenth century), female servants would be able to identify with the mood and concerns expressed in them. The epistles touch on a major problem of the time – communication with close family in geographically distant areas – and Whitney conveniently avoids repeated references to her identity as a writer. (In 'The Auctor to the Reader' she identifies herself as an ex-servant.) 'The Wyll and Testament,' the third major part of the *Nosegay* collection, would have attracted the mercantile population of the growing metropolitan city.

These were probably matters considered by any professional writer. But a female writer who wanted to reach a wide audience was faced with basic problems. If she wished to be taken seriously, she had to establish credibility with her audience, and this usually meant employing strategies to manoeuvre her way around cultural assumptions and restrictions. These strategies, of course, ultimately determined style. Indeed, the *Nosegay* is a very good example of how professional writing relates to gender, how strategies for establishing credibility and acceptance for commercial purposes intertwine with strategies for fending off criticism linked to the author's sex.

One of the striking characteristics of the *Nosegay* is the author's constant attention to the reader. Whitney opens the book with 'The Auctor to the Reader,' proceeds with 'T.B. in commendation of the Authour,' and concludes the first section with 'A Farewell to the Reader.' This repeated attention to her audience must be taken together with the fact that in both the dedication and the address to the reader she speaks as though the entire volume would be occupied with the 'philosophical flowers.' Although there is a possibility that Whitney and the printer changed plans and decided later to include 'Certain familier Epistles' and 'The Wyll and Testament' in the *Nosegay* book, it is equally possible that this is a strategy for acceptance. After all, she is writing a 'moral' book. This excessive concern with the reader indicates that she is trying to convince him or her of something.

Perhaps one of the things Whitney is trying to convince the reader about is herself and her work. The inclusion of 'T.B. in commendation of the Authour' helps her to do just that. By including this epistle, Whitney manages to declare herself a poet without transgressing to the point of advertising directly her own poetic talent. 'T.B. in commendation of the Authour' rests on the assumption that commendation is needed. And since T.B. is apparently a male (he signs 'Tho. Bir.' and spells 'Berrie' in the last stanza), it suggests further that commendation from a man is a certification of qualification for a profession which was closed to women. Accordingly, T.B. offers Whitney's work as a justification for recognizing women poets:

> To decke the wight, that worthie praises is:
>> and sure my great good wyll must never slake
> From WHITNEY: loe, herein some partie take
>> For in her worke is plainly to be seene,
>> Why Ladies place in Garlands Laurell greene.
>
> (B1r)

The implication here is that Whitney needs to be elevated specifically as a woman writer. But the elevation does not exceed socially accepted limits. It voices cultural biases regarding genre and gender:

42

She doth not write the brute or force in Armes,
Nor pleasure takes, to sing of others harmes,

But mustred hath and wrapped in a packe
a heape of Flowers of Philosophie:

The smelling flowers of an Arrbor sweete,
An Orcharde pickt presented is to thee:
And for her seconde worke, she thought it meete,
sithe Maides with loftie stile may not agree:

(B1v)

T.B. seems to deprecate, rather ambiguously, male (epic) authors who sing of the 'force in Armes' but at the same time he affirms the notion that even talented women are restricted to literary styles which agree with the rank of their sex. Like T.B.'s letter, the dedication of the work to a man (George Mainwaring) could serve as a credit to the author, a credit no less useful than any financial reward she might have looked forward to.

Included in the strategies for establishing credibility in the *Nosegay* is the deployment of contemporary dominant ideology, a strategy we have seen Whitney use in *A Copy of a Letter*. In several parts of her work Whitney appears to echo contemporary notions regarding proper feminine behaviour. Such a strategy not only guarantees her a sympathetic audience but also permits her to pass to the reader unorthodox ideas which might otherwise be rejected. When she tells her sister A.B. 'til some houshold cares mee tye,/ My bookes and Pen I wyll apply' (full passage quoted on p.39–40), she pays tribute to the conventional idea that a woman's principal place is in the home looking after her husband and her household, but at the same time she is presenting writing as an alternative profession (even though temporary) and that is a revolutionary idea in the middle decades of the sixteenth century. Likewise, she echoes contemporary dicta about restrained speech, but she applies them to both sexes, as in the moral adages, 105–7.

There is no doubt that as a woman writing in the 1570s, Whitney was working within narrow limits. It is difficult to say how conscious she was of the narrowness of space for expression, or to what extent she had internalized the cultural dicta she echoes in her work. Her letter to her friend 'Master T.L.' shows her to be aware of her culture's high regard for marriage and the consequent pressure on single people of both sexes to marry, but her advice seems grounded in experience rather than principle:

> But this I wish that you my frind
>   go chuse some vertues wife:
> With whom in feare of God do spend,
>   the residue of your lyfe
> For whylst you are in single state
>   none hath that right regard:
> They think all wel which they can win,
>   and compt it their reward.
>
>   (C3r)

The same can be said about the advice Whitney gives to her 'yonger Sisters servinge in London.' Her letter to them echoes middle-class, conduct-book regulations regarding speech and mood, but it is primarily a practical piece of advice, characterized by its emphasis on daily chores (like bolting doors before bedtime) and its procedure-like style. Conformity for social survival seems to be the message in both of these letters. How much of this conformist attitude stems from conviction and how much of it is actually a positive tactic to avoid friction with the 'spiteful' ones in her culture? Her own attempts to be a writer of secular literature in a culture which was hostile to such female creative activity as well as her earlier assertions in *The Copy of a Letter*, the first published criticism of men by an Englishwoman, negate conformism. But so many strategies interfere with so many issues that given the information we have at present it is impossible to come to a definitive conclusion.

MARGARET TYLER: ASSERTING WOMEN'S RIGHT TO LITERATURE

Almost unanimously, sixteenth-century theoreticians condemned romances as reading material for both sexes, and especially for women. In the *Instruction of a Christian Woman* (published in a translation by Richard Hyrde in 1529) Vives prohibits among other amorous material 'those ungracious books, such as be in my country in Spain.'[15] Concurring with Vives, Thomas Salter criticizes fathers who allow their daughters 'to come and learn by heart bookes, ballads, songes, sonnettes and dities of daliance, excityng their memories thereby.'[16] In the eyes of the moralists, romances and other types of books dealing with the subject of love could corrupt the minds of the people and especially of young women. Therefore, in their view, such material threatened to subvert the type of social morality they were trying to propagate. And the fears of the moralists mounted as more women, unmindful of what they were told, actually read the type of literature these men branded immoral.[17]

One woman, the ex-servant Margaret Tyler,[18] went beyond reading such literature. In 1578, about midway between Isabella Whitney's *Copy of a Letter* and Jane Anger's *Protection for Women*, Tyler published her translation of Diego Ortuñez de Calahorra's chivalric romance, *The Mirrour of Princely deedes and Knighthood*.[19] Advanced in years when she translated Ortuñez's book, Tyler made a mark both in the history of romantic fiction and in women's literary history. With a command of Spanish that was rare even among educated men of her time, Tyler set a mode in translating romances from the peninsular group, directly from the original language.[20] Following the publication of Tyler's translation, chivalresque romances became very popular in England, as they had been on the continent, and they were translated at a rapid rate.[21] The *Mirrour* was one of the most popular and influential, though it was not necessarily recognized as superior in merit to others in the same group.[22] It went through several editions, and authors like Spenser, Shakespeare, and Bunyan are said to have borrowed plot material from it.[23] The most radical aspect of Tyler's publication is the Preface she prefixed to her translation, a kind of feminist manifesto that marks its author as a distinct voice among her female contemporaries.

Tyler's Preface

Tyler's 'M.T. to the Reader' constitutes a landmark in feminist literary history on account of its being both the boldest criticism of patriarchal ideology by a woman writer up to that time[24] and one of the very few female-authored documents before the eighteenth century to deal with the problems of the literary woman whose imaginative voice is inhibited by patriarchal divisions of genre and gender. The Preface, which has attracted some attention,[25] is a defence of the translation of the *Mirrour* with reference to dominant notions about literature and gender. The following excerpt captures, I believe, most of the important points:

> Such delivery as I have made I hope thou wilt friendly accept, the rather for that it is a woman's work, though in a story prophane, and a matter more manlike then becometh my sexe. But as for the manlinesse of the matter thou knowest that it is not necessary for every trumpettour or drumstare in the warre to be a good fighter. . . . So Gentle Reader if my travaile in Englishing this Authour, may bring thee to a liking of the vertues heerin commended, and by example therof in thy princes & countries quarrel to hazard thy person & purchase good name, as for hope of well deserving my selfe that way, I neither bend my selfe therto nor yet feare the speach of people if I be found backward. . . . yet to report of armes is not so odious but that it may be borne withal, not onely in you men which your selves are fighters, but in us women, to whom the benefit in equal part apperteineth of your victories. . . . The invention, disposition, trimming, & what els in this story, is wholy an other mans, my part none therein but the translation. . . . So that the question now arriseth of my choice, not of my labour, wherefore I preferred this story before matter of more importance. . . . But my defence is by example of the best, amongst which many have dedicated their labours, some stories, some of warre, some phisick, some lawe, some as concerning government, some divine matters, unto diverse ladies & gentlewomen. And if men may & do bestow such of their travailes upon gentlewomen, then may we women read such of their works as they dedicate unto us, and if we may read them, why not farther wade in them to the serch of a truth. . . . if women be excluded from the view of such workes as appeare in their name, or if glory onely be sought in our common inscriptions, it mattereth not whether the parties be men or women, whether alive or dead. But to retourn whatsomever the truth is, whether that women may not at al discourse in learning, for men lay in their claim to be sole possessioners of knowledge, or whether they may in some maner that is by limitation or appointment in some kinde

of learning, my perswasion hath bene thus, that it is all one
for a woman to pen a story, as for a man to addresse his
story to a woman. But amongst al my il willers, some I hope
are not so straight that they would enforce me necessarily
either not to write or to write of divinitie.

(Sigs A3–A4)[26]

Tyler here exposes a number of cultural prohibitions and
general assumptions that were mostly implied in the apologies
of other women writers. One of these assumptions is that
'manlike' literature (i.e., literature whose subject matter deals
with martial affairs) is not appropriate for women. Implied in
this is the idea inherited from classical times that women are too
delicate and lightminded to deal with weighty matters, such as
war battles, and that they cannot speak about a subject they have
no experience in. (This calls to mind Whitney's 'commendator,'
Thomas Berrie, who praises her work but explains that 'she doth
not write the brute or force in Armes.') Another assumption
foregrounded here is the idea of learning as a male prerogative:
women 'may not at al discourse in learning,' for learning belongs
to men; only they can possess discursive knowledge. If women
are finally allowed to learn, they must be limited to 'some kinde
of learning.'

Tyler refutes these assumptions voiced a year later by the
conservative Thomas Salter,[27] and defends her work. In the first
half of the Preface she seems to answer anticipated charges that
the *Mirrour*, as a book that recounts battle scenes, is outside
a woman's territory, that the subject is 'more manlike then
becometh [her] sexe.' She takes issue with this restriction by
arguing that lack of experience in a subject does not preclude
writing about it, that men themselves write about things they
have never actively pursued. And even if it were 'bolde to
intermeddle in armes, so as the auncient Amazons did, and
in this story Claridiana doth,' she argues, women should not
be forbidden to write about battles which, though fought by
men, pertain to both sexes. In the second half of the Preface,
Tyler appears to answer anticipated criticism about the secular
nature of her book. Somewhat evasive about the exact object of
her defence, she attempts to explain why she has translated a
secular piece of literature. Her main point is that if men can
dedicate their works, of whatever subject, to women, then the

latter must be allowed to read them. And if they are allowed to read them, why shouldn't they be allowed to study and translate them? She points to the absurdity of the prohibition when she says that if women are barred from studying the works dedicated to them, 'it mattereth not whether the parties be men or women, whether alive or dead.' In this way Tyler exposes her culture's contradictions and biases in the ideology of gender. By dedicating his work to woman, man defines his actions in terms of her and her ability to appreciate them, applaud them, and reward them financially. His material and egotistic needs make him solicit her support. But he is not willing to relinquish his power over her, so he creates a contradictory state wherein he places restrictions on female activity, but not such as would hamper his own pursuits.

Tyler's defensive tactic is not always direct. Her slight evasiveness about the subject of the book betrays her uneasiness despite her bold statements, and calls attention once again to the difficulty in speaking out openly. The *Mirrour* is as much about love as it is about battles and Tyler knows it. But she seems to avoid referring directly to the subject of love. Early in the Preface she refers to the subject of the book as 'a story prophane' (non-religious) and later on calls it just a 'story.'[28] She defends her right to translate such a one, but she does not specify the aspects that make it controversial. Her comments on the book she translates focus on its didactic and entertaining nature:

> The chiefe matter therein contained is of exploits of wars, and the parties therein named, are especially renowned for their magnanimitie and courage. The authors purpose appeareth to be this, to animate thereby, and to set on fire the lustie courages of young gentlemen. . . . I doubt not gentle reader, but if it shal plese thee after serious matters to sport they self with this Spaniard, that thou shalt finde in him the just reward of mallice and cowardice, with the good speed of honesty and courage . . . so shalt thou have this stranger an honest man when neede serveth, and at other times, either a good companion to drive out a wery night, or a merry jest at thy boord.[29]
>
> (A3–A4)

Such notions could serve to legitimate her work. After all, the idea of literature for instruction and entertainment was not new.

Sidney was later to incorporate it in his *Apology for Poetry*, where he refers to *Amadis*, one of the romances on which the *Mirrour* is modelled, as capable of moving a reader's heart 'to the exercise of courtesie, liberalitie and especially courage.' Spenser worked with the same idea and so did many other Renaissance authors.

The Mirrour of Knighthood

Unlike most of the Preface, the text of the *Mirrour* is not radical. Nevertheless, it is critical of oppressive ideologies and cultural practices. The critique works indirectly, as in most women-authored texts, through a series of appropriations. While sometimes specific characters are set to voice opposition to oppressive structures, usually particular areas of culture are contested by endorsement of other conventional areas or by appeal to higher ideals. The *Mirrour* also opposes sixteenth-century cultural practice by following the chivalric code of justice, which contrasts with the one prevailing in the real world.

As Tyler's *Mirrour* is not available in a modern English edition, I shall provide a brief summary of its plot before turning to an analysis of the text itself. In the monastery of the river lives the beautiful princess Briana, at a distance from her parents' court. Her father, the emperor of Hungary, has waged war of expansion on Greece. But he is militarily not strong enough, so he makes an alliance with the British king. The terms of the alliance are: 20,000 troops and the personal help of the British king's son, Edward, in exchange for the hand of the Princess Briana. So Briana, daughter of the king of Hungary, is to marry Edward, son of the king of Great Britain. The two have never met. But the plans become thwarted. The emperor of Greece, against whom Edward is to fight, falls in love with Briana's reported beauty. So on the way to the monastery of the river he kills Edward and presents himself to Briana as Prince Edward, with documents and all. Briana and Trebatio (alias Edward) are married by the archbishop in the monastery. Briana has been advised by her father not to consummate her marriage before her husband goes to war, but she disobeys his advice. She becomes pregnant, and Trebatio disappears, not to go to war but in search of the enchanted chariot which in his dreams has carried off Briana. She gives birth to two sons who become the

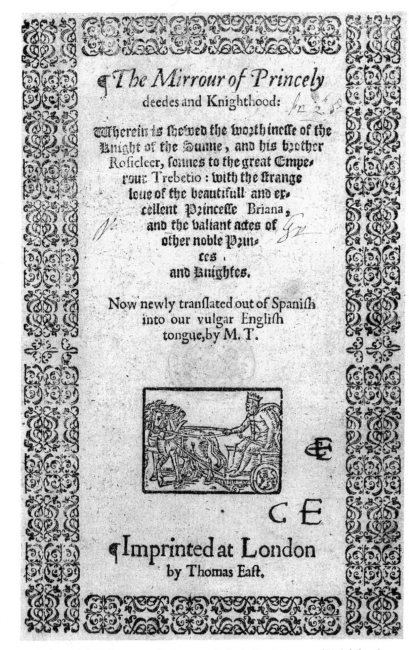

¶The Mirrour of Princely
deedes and Knighthood:

Wherein is shewed the worthinesse of the
Knight of the Sunne, and his brother
Rosicleer, sonnes to the great Emperour Trebetio: with the strange
loue of the beautifull and excellent Princesse Briana,
and the valiant actes of
other noble Prin-
ces.
and Knightes.

Now newly tranflated out of Spanish
into our vulgar English
tongue, by M. T.

¶Imprinted at London
by Thomas Eaft.

Figure 2.2 Title page of Margaret Tyler's *The Mirrour of Knighthood*
(London: T. East, 1578).

narrative's new heroes. One of the sons is named Rosicleer, the other Donzel del Febo (or Knight of the Sun). From a very young age, each of the two disappears separately from the mother's abode in the monastery of the river. They search for adventure and their father. They travel far and wide in Asia, Africa, and Europe, performing deeds of chivalry. They rescue women and reinstate the dispossessed. Rosicleer falls in love with Olivia, daughter of the king of Great Britain, and she with him. The affair is secret and Olivia is worried, for Rosicleer's birth is of doubtful origin. Her father intends to marry her off to an heir of a neighbouring state. Matters are pending. Meanwhile, after twenty years, Trebatio returns to the monastery of the river. He gives explanations for his absence and he is glad to find his wife waiting for him. Deciding not to introduce himself to her father, he elopes with her to Greece.

Like other sixteenth-century chivalric romances, *The Mirrour* combines courtly and chivalric elements with Renaissance ideas on love, marriage, and sexual conduct. As the setting and structure of the plot clearly derive from the chivalric tradition, so do the ideals which the book upholds. The heroes are carried to distant parts of the world through a series of adventures which purport to prove their courage and honour. They are possessed of superhuman strength and fight endless battles against giants or others who exploit the disadvantaged through sheer physical force. At least one of the two major love relationships in the book is conducted according to the concept of male service inherited from courtly love. At the same time, the male/female relationships clearly show that love is allied to marriage and so is sex. Olivia is distressed to find out that the man she loves may not be eligible as a husband, and Briana can experience sexual intercourse only when she is married; and even then she has to appear modest and relatively passive. (We are told that she consents 'somewhat against her will,' because Trebatio is after all 'hir lawfull husband,' ch. 7, p. 12r.) Sexual passion and expression of sexual desire is an attribute of the man.

These elements do not harmoniously coexist in the text. Restrictions and differences in conduct become especially pronounced as they are set against an ideal tradition that allowed total mutuality in the heterosexual love relationships and that recognized a more equitable exercise of power between the sexes. At the same time, certain ideologies and cultural practices, which conflict with human desires and which obtained in Renaissance society, are contested. The *Mirrour* undermines and at times repudiates sixteenth-century ideology and cultural practice in at least three areas: marriage and class; the double standard; and women and violence.

In the sixteenth century, marriage theory and practice were based on the need of the aristocratic class to maintain its power through inheritance. Although in earlier utopian social theory, members from different castes might be allowed to marry, nowhere else was such a practice encouraged. The conflict that resulted from the individual's desire to marry for love and the tragic consequences of disinheritance can be attested by many an example in Renaissance literature, especially in drama. The socio-political changes that took place in the transition from feudal to early modern state necessitated regulation of membership in a hereditary nobility – hence also the increase in the concern over legitimacy of birth. Marriages were based on alliances made between families with titles to property. This was, of course, especially true of the aristocracy and the bourgeoisie, since clearly the lower classes had little to bargain over. Despite humanistic ideas about love and marriages, material considerations prevailed in matches among the nobility. Property and political alliance remained the most important criteria in the marriages of the upper classes.[30] Through the threat of disinheritance, the parents had power over whom their children would marry. Often marriages would be arranged when the children were still very young. And legal practice supported the parents' power, for parental consent was required by law for most marriages. Theory supported cultural practice in this respect and the material motive of the aristocracy was coupled with the Renaissance concern to establish the patriarchal family. Middle-class conduct manuals emphasized marriage within one's social rank and often interpreted a woman's desire to marry someone of lower class as an attempt on her part to gain control over the man. (William Googe, for example, speaks of the arrogance of some women in marrying men of lower rank.)[31] The *Mirrour* seems to undermine several of these ideas and practices. It shows the utter incompatability between love and material marriage and challenges very strongly barriers of caste. Interestingly, the text views this matter mainly, though not solely, from a female perspective and shows the binds that women are placed in when they are treated as commodities.

Two parts of the narrative, the story of Briana and Trebatio and that of Olivia and Rosicleer, show the binds of class and gender and finally affirm the primacy of love. Trebatio is not a chivalric hero, but he seems to uphold some chivalric ideals. He stands against imperialism and for love without bargains. Attracted to the reported beauty of Briana, he kills his materialistic adversary Edward, vowing that 'although thou wast mine enemie and come in favour of the kinge Tiberio to take from me my land and high estate, yet woulde I not have bene so cruel an enimie unto thee, but that entire love of the princesse Briana drave me more therto, then mine owne enmitie' (ch. 9, p. 15r). Edward is the one who has accepted woman (Briana) as a tradable commodity. He has come to buy her with his 20,000 men and his military skill in her father's expansionist enterprises. Trebatio too displays a certain degree of aggression in claiming Briana. He also treats her as his prerogative, and in this respect he is more a Renaissance male than a chivalric hero. But he at least does not participate in the system that puts a price on women and uses them as pawns in military alliances.

Briana is presented in conventionally acceptable terms. In *Amadis* and other romances of the same type, the leading female character disobeys or deceives her father in her decision to follow her lover.[32] In the *Mirrour*, Briana is made to appear much less deceitful and rebellious, at least on the surface. Trebatio's disguise as Edward frees her from the responsibility of disobeying her father's will.[33] In fact her initial recognition of filial duty and obedience would have been applauded by any sixteenth-century theorist on female conduct:

> I will accomplish that which the duetie of obedience unto the king my father forceth me unto, for that I must subject my wil unto his commaundement, yet I so consider of this your offer and request, as that from this time I will dare to compare with you in like happinesse.

> (ch. 6, p. 10v)

But her last statement in this passage would not have been applauded, for it implies a little too much forwardness and hope for equality. Equally troubling would be her decision at the beginning of the book to consummate her 'marriage' and at the end to elope with Trebatio to Greece. Here the portrayal of an ostensibly dutiful and virtuous daughter supports the woman's sexual responsiveness and her final act of disobedience.

The union between Trebatio and Briana is not a case of expediency, and the story itself reads like an example of how to thwart an arranged marriage. We are shown that the Trebatio–Briana marriage succeeds because the material motives attendant on the original match between Briana and Edward have been removed. The narrative is constructed so that the reader will approve the change in circumstances. It is important to note here that Edward's replacement is rendered necessary not by the plot but by his materialistic motives, which preclude him as a candidate for the role of chivalric hero.

Furthermore, the Briana–Trebatio relationship may be seen as oppositional also on account of its conventional elements. Briana is presented in a way which accentuates her characteristics as a *feme covert*. Her geographical isolation may be part of the romance convention, but her seclusion does not become any less real. This seclusion inadvertently serves as a symbol for the condition of sixteenth-century women and their exclusion from the public sphere, the world of action. She is a woman who is acted upon by men and who has very little control over what happens to her. Even the man who loves her leaves her pregnant and disappears for twenty years. She has to live a life of patience and pain, trying to hide her children in order to prevent social disgrace. This is a sympathetic representation which tends to accentuate the disadvantages of a woman in cultural terms and hence holds the potential of eliciting identification from the female reader and awakening realization of oppression – 'look what happens to us women.' At the end, like a faithful Penelope, Briana gets her man back, but the narrative does not in any way imply that this fact justifies the pain she undergoes. And even if it did, the potential for identification could not be erased. In fact, as I discuss later, it shows that Trebatio owes some explanations about his actions. This is unlike the sort of thing that one finds in books like *Penelope's Web* (1587) where obedience, chastity, and silence are not only expected but taken for granted.[34]

The Olivia–Rosicleer affair in the book likewise undermines sixteenth-century theory and practice with regard to marriage and caste. Here Don Silverio, a less crude version of Edward, is the representative of the status quo who serves as antagonist to the chivalric hero, Rosicleer. Like Edward, Don Silverio appears ready to claim the benefits that the traditional system of marriage offers to men of his title and social position. More confident about his material assets than his love for Olivia, he comes to ask for her in marriage, 'presuming upon his byrth and livelihood that she should be graunted unto him' (ch. 32, p. 83r). Olivia's father, King Oliverio, supports this system of marriage as political property alliance. He attempted such an alliance when he sent his son Edward to Hungary, and now he tries it with the marriage of his daughter. He explains to her why Don Silverio is a good match:

> [He is] a comly knight of personage, valiant in armes, of a couragious spirite above, all vertuous, and in his dealinges circumspect, courteous of speach and of highe estate. . . . Ther are besides to commend this match the entercourse of trafficke betweene our subjectes, and the friendshippe betweene his parents and mee.
>
> (ch. 55, p. 177v)

This type of marriage is a self-reproducing system within the propertied class. The *Mirrour* shows the restrictions that this system imposes on women especially, and through Olivia criticizes the values of the class that upholds it. Olivia is first set up as a supporter of aristocratic practices and values but is soon turned into a critical opponent of these. Caught between her love for Rosicleer and what she believes to be the barrier of class between them, she makes the most eloquent case in favour of abolishing noble birth as a criterion for marriage within the aristocratic class. Her speech, a long discursive passage within the narrative, is one of the most important statements in a book translated by a woman and largely read by members of her sex:

> What a wicked world is this, wherein men of force must neglect other mens vertues, and magnifie their owne nobilitie wythout deserte: were it not more reason to rayse this man to the toppe of honour that in him his posteritie may glory, then for lacke of auncestors famous for like qualities, to suppresse his vertue and keepe under the magnanimitie of his courage? When began my fathers and grandfathers to be nobles, but when with the winges

of vertue they soared above the vulgar sort, and if by their meanes onely I am advaunced to be a Princesse, what thancke is there to mee of my highnesse? and thou Rosicleer if by those rare and sovereygne vertues . . . thou dost mount in credit . . . art not thou worthy of greater renowne then we others whych clymbing by vertue in lyke sorte, never yet came to the possibylytie of like worthinesse? Is not this a forgery of the world and a playne ingling wyth nobility, when we must make more account of one which perhaps by disorder of life defaceth the honour of his race, then of one which reacheth by the ignobilitie of his stocke, wherein consisteth nobilitye in the opinion of men, or in vertue in deede? and doo men inherit vertue as the chylde entereth uppon the fathers lande beeinge lawfull heyre? No, heere wee receyve naught but what our selves sowe, and hee that reapeth not maye be a loute for all his Lordshippe, as in tyme appeareth, whiche judgeth freely and wythout affection. And for mee, if the eyes of my understandinge were not dymmed, I shoulde soone confesse lesse merite in me to deserve Rosicleer then wanteth in him to bee worthy of me. . . . But sith of force I must yeelde to the time and rather dye then acknowledge the contrary, *sith my Fortune is such that I must live by the immagination of other men*, and sith my estate may not be yoked with hys basenesse, have at it, I will for ever shutte him from my presence for the savegard of myne honour.

(ch. 39, pp. 114r–114vs; emphasis added)

This passage and indeed most of chapter 39 is very similar in spirit to Tyler's Preface. Both deal with restrictions on women, one focusing on gender, the other on class. Both show the binds that culture and class place on women. In this bind the *Mirrour* encourages the choice of love, for the narrative is set up so that the reader will approve Olivia's final decision to accept Rosicleer's supposed low birth.

The *Mirrour*'s opposition to dominant ideology is also evident in its criticism of the double standard. The strongest and most articulate objection is raised with regard to adultery. One of the feats of the Knight of the Sun, brother of Rosicleer, is the defence of the Duchess Elisandra, who has been accused of adultery and dispossessed of her property. The Knight of the Sun and his father Trebatio are on their way to the monastery of the river when they hear the cries of distressed gentlewomen. The latter are representatives of Elisandra, Duchess of Pannonia. Married for eight years, Elisandra has no children. Her husband, fearing that in the absence of children her inheritance would revert to her kin, accuses her of adultery to get rid of her. To present his case convincingly, he makes one of his friends (Arydon) his accomplice. The whole scheme is described as follows:

> For a plot of ground adjacent to his segniories, his accusation lyeth thus that with himselfe [Arydon] she committed adultery. . . . The Duke presently complaineth to the king, and both partyes are sent for in all hast. Arydon being first asked confesseth it, and is acquitted by his confession. *As (by the way) our lawe in this case acquiteth the man once confessing it though otherwise never so great an offender, and onely stretcheth to the woman in respect of hir faythe given at marriage.*
>
> (ch. 50, p. 166v; emphasis added)

The only hope of this woman, we are told, is to find a knight who will defend her innocence in a battle with the mighty Arydon. The Knight of the Sun undertakes the task, and in the ensuing battle, which takes place in the presence of the king and other judges, kills Arydon, who at the last minute confesses his part in the Duke's plot against his wife. The Duke is ordered to be executed, and the story ends by abolishing the double standard in the law governing adultery:

> For albeit many of his nobles entreated for their pardon, yet the king so abhorred the villany that nought availed: and at this time was the lawe first enacted in Hungary that *the law of punnishment for whoredome should stretche aswell to the man as to the woman*, and that, *equall penaltie* should be assigned to lyke offendours, whereas before the men escaped the women onely were in danger.
>
> (ch. 54, p. 175r; emphasis added)

The bias in the law described in the above two passages is not much different from that which existed in most countries of sixteenth-century Europe, including England. Such passages show, among other things, that where matters of sexuality were concerned, the law assumed the innocence of the man and the guilty part of the woman. They also show how closely linked the interests of patriarchy were with the legal rights of women and how sexuality could be manipulated at the expense of the female sex. The change of the law as suggested in the passage could only occur in fiction, of course. In reality, legal changes could not be effected so easily.

In the sixteenth century the double standard in sexual conduct was widespread. Fidelity in the marriage was in theory required of both men and women, but only women were morally condemned for their lack of chastity. A Penelope was expected to remain faithful, but a wandering Ulysses could have several sexual escapades in his travels. Western literary tradition reinforced the double standard by giving the hero, married or not, complete freedom in his sexual behaviour. The chivalric romance, as a form which derived from the epic, kept several of its conventions, the sexual enchantment of the hero among them. But the chivalric code, which the romance likewise incorporated, required fidelity from both lovers. The *Mirrour* registers the disparity between the two traditions, a disparity made especially apparent by the author's attempts to provide excuses for Trebatio's behaviour. When Trebatio, a married man, becomes enchanted in the Castle of Lindaraza (the equivalent of Acrasia's Bower of Bliss in Spenser's *Faerie Queene*), apologies are offered to the reader:

> And you must pardon the Emperour if by this he was wholy possessed with hir [Lindaraza's] love, and forgot his late wife the Princesse Briana.
>
> (ch. 9, p. 16v)

His enchantment, we are told further, was due to 'the secreate of the place.' He was 'deprived of his understanding,' in a state of semi-consciousness or 'sweet sleep' (ch. 9, p. 16v). When he finally returns to Briana in the monastery of the river, she is made to ask:

> My Lorde and onely lyfe what cruell Fortune hath detayned you from this lande, and bannished you so long from my presence.
>
> (ch. 51, p. 169r)

To which Trebatio replies:

58

Madame . . . you may call that Fortune cruell, for it hath offered you a great wronge by forceing you to endure a farre greater penaunce then Penelope dyd by Ulysses absence: but one thinge you maye assure your selfe of that the fault was not in mee thoughe I am not to bee excused, for if I had had lyfe and lybertie and judgement, all the world should not have stayed me from you.

Since my freedome if I have not had as loyall a regarde of your constancye and my duetie, then blame all mankinde for my sake of unstedfastnesse and wronge, and for this tyme let these things slippe wyth lesse griefe to entertayne our present joye.

(ch. 51, pp. 169r–169v)

However naïve-sounding, such passages clearly imply that apologies are needed, that Trebatio's lack of constancy cannot be presented as an assumed right. They also have the effect of legitimating opposition to the double standard.

As mentioned earlier, the *Mirrour* does not advocate the type of sexual equality that was found in the courtly love romances of the twelfth century. Sexual modesty is an attribute of the female character mainly, although it is occasionally found in the male one also. (Rosicleer, for example, shows abashedness when he faces Olivia in public after he has fallen in love with her, ch. 34, p. 96v.) But the fact remains that the *Mirrour* foregrounds and criticizes at least the crude forms of the double standard just discussed.

The *Mirrour* also foregrounds the issue of violence against women. It reiterates throughout the chivalric rule that it is a crime to use violence on a woman. And in so far as violence against women includes also violence against her will, the defence of women on this account runs counter to sixteenth-century theory and cultural practice which fostered such violence. It is of course one of the conventions in chivalric romances for the hero to seek adventures and to try to right the wronged. But in the *Mirrour* the victims, which the heroes succour, are almost always women. In the course of the book there are no less than eight incidents in which women come running for help because they are threatened by rape, forced marriage, or disinheritance. Two of them are particularly interesting and I shall recount them briefly.

The first concerns one Arguirosa, heir to the kingdom of Thessaly. Her father married a woman of questionable character. When he died, his widow married her lover Rolando, who seizes the throne by force, excluding Arguirosa, the rightful heir. Rolando is physically a strong man and his kinsmen are of the same sort. Arguirosa is powerless. 'But that which is worst of all was, that to undoe hir rightefull claime, hee mindeth to marrye hir with a kinsman of his and to give [her] onely some lyttle towne to dwell in' (ch. 47, p. 157v). Arguirosa has come to the tournaments at the British king's court hoping to find a knight who will undertake her quarrel.

The second incident also involves an heiress but the offence is even more personal. Princess Radamira is the 'inheritress' of Cyprus. Raiartes, a great giant, hears of her beauty and comes to her island to demand her for his wife. Her father refuses and Raiartes kills him in a duel. Through sheer strength, Raiartes takes over her property, carries her against her will to his country, and forces her to accept him as husband. Radamira, 'abhoring nothing so much as the company of Raiartes,' finally makes a deal with him: if she finds a knight who will defeat Raiartes in battle, she will be set at liberty. Thus Radamira rides through the courts of Europe to find a knight who will undertake her cause.

The first of these incidents involves mainly loss of title and property while the second concerns loss of personal freedom as well. Both incidents are embedded in a patriarchal society. The power clearly belongs to the men while the women are not so much weak as powerless. Such incidents involving loss of inheritance and forced marriage were commonplace in the sixteenth century and earlier. The difference was that in actual life there was no court to which women could appeal in order to defend their cause. Not only that, but Renaissance legal and social practice formally brought under the man's control the very rights which are defended by the chivalric heroes here. A woman could be forced through the threat of disinheritance to accept a husband she disliked and her right to property could be manipulated by the male heirs. (The case of Lady Anne, Countess of Clifford is one obvious example.) The *Mirrour* reaffirms the restitution of women's legal rights. Even in chivalry, however, such feats are exceptional, for the wrong-doers are almost always possessed of enormous physical strength and superhuman abilities are needed to overcome them. Rosicleer and his brother are no ordinary mortals. But the fact that the *Mirrour* undertakes the defence of such issues on any level constitutes in itself an act of opposition to dominant ideology and practice. And it is important to notice that the text prioritizes the issues on which women must be defended: whims are not treated seriously.[35]

These are the direct and indirect expressions of opposition to sixteenth-century dominant ideology and social practice. The absences from the text are equally important. There is first an absence of any language that denotes subordination. It is true that sexual modesty is mainly a female characteristic. But there is nothing which explicitly states the idea of a woman's subordination to man. In this respect the *Mirrour* keeps the chivalric code, which does not permit such inferior status for women. There is also an overall absence of stereotyped views of women. In the very few instances where they occur, they are disproven by the narrative itself. Olivia, for example, reproaches herself in terms traditionally used against her sex ('O inconstant and frayle womankinde . . . lyght in beliefe, light in judgement,' ch. 41, p. 130r). But the narrative shows that she does not deserve such self-reproach since she has good reasons to worry about her lover's social rank. Moreover, Olivia criticizes herself and is not censured by others.

There is also an overall absence of the type of adjectives that describe women as dainty and coy. None of the female characters in the *Mirrour* is endowed with these traditionally feminine attributes. The portrait of the Amazon Claridiana in chapter 45 may be revealing in this respect. Claridiana, daughter of the queen of the Amazons, first appears chasing a wild boar. Three knights happen to see her and they are awestruck by her grace, and beauty particularly, but 'the Lady more bolde then the men' wakes them up as it were with a blow on her horn. Introductions are made and courtesies are exchanged. Meanwhile Claridiana's entourage (consisting of thirty gentlewomen and thirty or more male knights) arrives, but not before she has had a chance to devise a trick she will play on her knights both for her amusement and for that of the strangers. The jest is finally revealed, and she invites the three new knights to her parents' court where she is shortly to be knighted. The combination of beauty and masculine skill (in hunting) that Claridiana displays are probably commonplace attributes in representations of warrior women, and so too might be the description of her atypical upbringing and heritage. (She was trained in hunting, we are told, since early youth and her mother 'achieved such enterprises that in hir time there was no knight more famous.') But noticeably absent are those signs of feminity that Simon Shepherd notices in Spenser's *Faerie Queen* – Britomart's smock and hair revelation, and the 'dainty parts' in the encounter with Radimund.[36] Unless it were Claridiana's 'softe paces' (ch. 45, p. 141v), nothing else in the description implies traditional notions of femininity. In fact the roles seem somewhat reversed. It is the men who are unhelmeted and it is male beauty that is being revealed. The women are among the admirers: 'wherat smiling they all unbuckeled their helmets Bargandel and Liriamandro beeing then of the age of 20 yeares, seeming so beautifull that as well the gentlewomen as the knights were amazed at them' (ch. 45, pp. 151v–153r). Claridiana behaves with greater ease than the men. When they pay her a compliment, she returns one freely and displays, in addition to her skill in hunting, a natural playfulness, a sense of humour, and a freedom in movement and expression.

Conservative male translators would not have been likely to render faithfully such parts. Spanish literature was considered very liberal in its attitudes towards women, and men like Barnaby Googe did not hesitate to alter the original text so as to make it conform to a certain standard of sexual modesty.[37] Tyler did not expurgate her text. This fact as well as her mention of Claridiana in the Preface to refute traditional divisions of experience suggest that Tyler was approvingly conscious of the *Mirrour*'s oppositional tendencies.

3

NOBLEWOMEN DRAMATIZING THE HUSBAND–WIFE CONFLICT

'The Lady, shall we venture to say, turns out to be merely a wife,' states Ruth Kelso in the introduction to her well-documented study, *Doctrine for the Lady of the Renaissance*.[1] Indeed, Renaissance restrictions on women cut across all social classes. The curbing on speech and public appearance, for example, applied, with some modifications, as much to a countess as to any woman lower down the social scale. So a noblewoman wishing to publish a work of literature was not free to do so on account of her title and education.

In many ways she was more restricted because her actual life was more strictly regulated. For one thing, women in the aristocracy and the upper gentry exercised little control over whom they would marry; prestige, titles, and property were much too important to the fathers to leave them depending on the hearts of their young daughters. Secondly, noblewomen were usually married to men much older than themselves (and older than the norm in the population at large). So it was not unusual for an aristocrat's 13-year-old daughter to marry someone who was old enough to be her father or even her grandfather (the case of Mary Herbert). Such practices were likely to reinforce submissive and formal behaviour and to discourage personal assertion. Direct economic dependence may also have encouraged outward conformity, as there were no means of livelihood for a noblewoman once she had been turned out of doors by husband and parents (the case of Elizabeth Cary). In these respects noblewomen were distinguished from their social inferiors (to whom I broadly refer as sub-aristocratic). Among the middle and lower classes, daughters and wives had a greater say in matters that concerned them, often contributed to the family income and engaged in family quarrels.[2] This might explain why the women I study in this chapter seem more inclined than their sub-aristocratic counterparts to comply, at least on the surface, with the socially accepted norms of behaviour. Unlike Whitney and Tyler, who more or less claim their right to publish and rave against men, Lady Herbert and Lady Cary show reluctance to appear in print and to express their ideas openly. The reluctance to publish is a characteristic among upper-class writers of either sex, but here it is accompanied by signs of female modesty. Cary hides what she writes, and Herbert chooses to work through men. In their writings these women usually favour female characters who are only inoffensively assertive. Even the difference in the upbringing between Mary Herbert (née Sidney) and Elizabeth Cary (née Tanfield) – the former comes from a liberal family, the latter from a conservative one – is not enough to make a corresponding difference in freedom of expression. But the fact that these women can come forward at all at the time they do to publish secular literature may be largely explained by the influence of humanism. In the wide and influential humanist circles, women were prompted to engage in intellectual pursuits, and humanist men often served as advertisers of women's artistic talents.

MARY HERBERT: ENGLISHING A PURIFIED CLEOPATRA

In 1575, when she was 15, Mary Sidney entered an arranged mar-riage with the 50-year-old William Herbert, Earl of Pembroke. He was a humanist, patron of the arts, and one of the wealthiest aristocrats in England.[3] Her marriage apparently offered her a fair degree of freedom. Various references to her husband suggest that she may even have been the dominant one in the pair.[4] Two years after the wedding, young Mary followed her husband to the Pembroke residence at Wilton, the 'little court in the depths of the country.' From this post Mary Herbert played a prominent role in the cultural life of England for nearly a quarter of a century. Under her direction, Wilton became a literary centre, comparable to continental literary salons. Friends, literary acquaintances, and prospective protégés visited and sometimes stayed at Wilton to present their work, circulate manuscripts, partake in discussions, and even to watch theatrical performances.[5] The milieu included well-known authors like Daniel, Spenser, Ralegh, Jonson, and John Davies of Hereford, but also minor writers like Abraham Fraunce, Nicholas Breton, Gervase Babington, and Samuel Brandon. Lady Herbert patronized these and other men (though the number of authors to whom she paid more than a token fee has been exaggerated). After the death of her brother, Sir Philip Sidney, she devoted much time to editing and publishing his work. Her own literary accomplishments include several translations – Mornay's treatise *Discourse of Life and Death*, Garnier's play *Antonie*, Petrach's *Triumph of Death*; a versification of the Psalms, to which her brother Philip had also contributed; and a few original poems – 'A Dialogue between two shepheards,' 'The Dolefull Lay of Clorinda,' 'To the Angel spirit,' and 'Even now that Care.'[6]

As this activity shows, Mary Herbert was a woman of literary ambition. But the forms she used to express this ambition clearly suggest an indirect, self-effacing strategy. Her case tells an interesting story about the interplay between personal ambition and compliance with culturally constructed feminine roles. Extremely reluctant to display her talents, she usually worked from behind curtains, using men as protective shields. Significant men in her life became surrogate figures, public substitutes of her own creative self.

Her brother Philip was apparently one of these substitutes. Understandably, his premature death caused her a great deal of pain, especially as there had been a strong bond between them, made stronger still by common intellectual interests. But this tragic event was apparently also the catalyst for much creative energy, as nearly all of her works date from after his death (she was twenty-five when he died). She became preoccupied with editing and publishing the work he had left in manuscript form, and she tried to popularize his ideas. In her choice of subjects for translation she went to sources he had favoured. Even when she published some of her own work, she declared that she did it to honour her brother. This devotion was an expression of her love for him as well as a shield of protection from seeming to seek fame – a strictly unfeminine endeavour in her culture. A woman that published in her own name could be suspected of self-display. The sister of Sir Philip Sidney, the admired 'shepherd poet' of Elizabeth's court, could also be suspected of

Figure 3.1 Mary Sidney, Countess of Pembroke, an engraving by
Simon van der Passé, 1618.

trying to compete with her famous brother, to show that she was better. Public self-effacement becomes a way out of this bind. In the dedication of the Psalms to her brother, she apologizes for the inferiority of her own part of the translation. But in view of the many changes she introduced to improve her brother's phrasing in the part he versified,[7] her apologies stand in contrast to a privately expressed confidence in her own poetic ability, and point to a split between private and public expression.

Sometimes she hired male writers to do what sometimes she could have done better than they. Such members of her circle as Samuel Daniel, Nicholas Breton, and Abraham Fraunce were particularly instrumental in expressing her wishes and ideas. While she acted as a generous patron to these and other men, there was an unusual interdependence between herself and the authors she commissioned. The system of patronage, of course, by its very nature fostered such an interdependence. In seeking financial support and protection, an author often had to make compromises in what he wrote. But the Countess seems to have had an especially binding relationship with the authors she patronized. This is evidenced above all by the fact that she usually assigned works to her protégés.[8] The case of Samuel Daniel, under her patronage for many years, illustrates this relationship. Next to her brother, Daniel seems to have been the most important surrogate figure. Most of the works he dedicated to her were her assignments. His *Cleopatra* certainly and his 'Letter from Octavia' very probably were written as sequels to her translation of *Antonie*. Even his *Civil Wars* was a direct response to her wishes. The most suggestive evidence of the strong demands made by the Countess on Daniel is contained in his 'Funerall Poeme' which he wrote for his later patron, Charles Blount, Lord Mountjoy: 'Nor was it [Mountjoy's patronage] such, as could lay on me/ As t'inforce m'observance, beyond thee,/ Or make my conscience differ from my tongue.'[9] Daniel's need to articulate this point and the fact that he was impressed by Mountjoy's laxity probably suggest that under his previous patron he lacked complete freedom in writing.

While patronage offered Mary Herbert a way of channelling authorial creativity, it also became a kind of cultural trap for her, pushing her further into a conventional role. Prospective protégés fashioned her public image. Breton painted her portrait as a reflection of the Duchess of Urbino in Casteglione's *Courtier*:

'who hath redde of the Duchesse of Urbino, may saie, the Italians wrote well: but who knows the Countess of Pembroke, I think hath cause to write better.'[10] Many authors reinforced this image by commenting on her intellectual endowments, her generosity, the inspiration she imparted, and her noble task of making her brother's work known. Some even attributed a specific morality to her. In translating Tasso's *Aminta*, for example, Abraham Fraunce changed a love scene in a pastoral dialogue to conform to what he thought would be a tribute to the Countess. Unlike Tasso's heroine, Fraunce's Phillis refuses to let Aminta kiss her because without marriage this kind of love is not 'Discreate and sober.'[11] Likewise, Thomas Moffet, the physician and entomologist of the Pembroke circle, wrote a long poem on female silkworm moths as models of chastity, hoping to appeal to what he perceived to be the Countess's notions of sexual modesty.[12] These and other authors who sought the Countess's favours praised not only qualities that they saw in her but also those they thought she would wish to have. (Breton's vision of the Countess as a spiritual being who rejects all earthly things in his *Countesse of Pembrokes Love* is an excellent example of this.) In so doing, such authors contributed to constructing the Countess's identity as a pious and learned woman, at the same time as they reflected their culture's notions of respectable female conduct. This explains their emphasis on her role as patron rather than as author, despite her talent. Mary Herbert seems to have acquiesced in the construction of this identity, as Queen Elizabeth I accepted and reinforced the image of Gloriana, the Virgin Queen. But as in Queen Elizabeth's case, the constructed identity also became a kind of trap. The image of the pious, learned, and generous patroness inspired respect and raised her status but it also restricted her development as an author.

Remaining within this frame meant, among other things, very little direct writing and publishing. Indicatively, Mary Herbert worked almost exclusively in the area of translation. When she translated secular literature she stuck closely to the original text.[13] This shows how hesitant she was to appear assertive. To translate freely is to risk one's own interpretation. To translate literally is to seek protection in the idea of conveying the author's meaning exactly.

Antonie

Of Mary Herbert's several translations, the one that stands out as particularly interesting is that of Garnier's play *Antonie*, published in 1592. Literary critics have so far seen this play mainly in relation to Shakespeare's *Antony and Cleopatra* or to the Countess's attempt (or supposed attempt) to reform the English stage according to Sir Philip Sidney's dramatic precepts, expressed in his *Apology for Poetry*. Mary Herbert's devotion to her brother's ideals and Daniel's statement about chasing away 'Grosse Barbarisme' in his dedication of *Cleopatra* (*Antonie*'s sequel) have been cited as evidence that the play was intended as an attack on, or answer to, popular drama. Mary Ellen Lamb has contested this view, arguing that the Countess of Pembroke never thought of waging a battle against popular theatre and that her translation of Garnier's play sprung quite simply from her interest in *ars moriendi*, or the art of dying well.[14] My purpose here is not to engage in this debate but to focus on the translator's identity as a woman publishing a secular play in the sixteenth century.

Mary Herbert's choice of play for translation seems to indicate that while her forms of authorial expression may have been conservative, her ideas were not. Written in the French neo-Senecan tradition for an elite audience and intended for private reading rather than stage production, *Antonie* is characterized by its refined language and moral tone.[15] But whereas its form is thus restrained, and therefore suitable for a female translator like the Countess, its ideas and attitudes are bold and at times subversive in the context of sixteenth-century ideology and culture. The play interrogates conventional definitions of masculine and feminine virtue, opposes the established association of overt female sexuality with loose morals, and reveals the psychological and sexual complexes of those holding political power.

Antonie offers a sympathetic view of the adulterous lovers, and especially of Cleopatra, the woman who up to that time had been presented to the English public as a seductress.[16] Following a number of French and Italian contemporary versions, rather than Plutarch or the Roman authors, the play idealizes and conventionalizes its heroine according to sixteenth-century standards. First, it purifies her by purging her love from political motives and thus dissociates her from the image of the political conniver found in Plutarch and other sources. Unwavering in her loyalty to her lover, the heroine of *Antonie* never contemplates alliance with Caesar. Upon Antony's fall, the pragmatic Charmion, Cleopatra's woman, suggests:

> You see him ruin'd, so as your support
> No more henceforth can him with comfort raise.
> With-draw you from the storme: persist not still
> To loose your selfe: this royall diademe
> Regaine of Caesar.
>
> (ll. 529–33)[17]

Charmion's advice, however, only serves to highlight Cleopatra's idealism:

> *Cl.* Sooner shining light
> Shall leave the day, and darknes leave the night:
> Sooner moist currents of tempestuous seas
> Shall wave in heaven, and the nightly troopes
> Of starres shall shine within the foming waves,
> Then I thee, Antony, leave in deepe distres.
>
> (ll. 533–8)

In other sources the Egyptian queen's decision to commit suicide in the end is linked to various motives. Daniel's Cleopatra, for example, fears humiliation as a queen in the streets of Rome and as a woman in the eyes of Octavia.[18] In contrast, Garnier's heroine tries to prove, almost single-mindedly, her loyalty to her lover:

> Die Cleopatra then, no longer stay
> From Antony, who thee at Styx attends:
> Go joyne thy Ghost with his, and sob no more
> Without his love within these tombes enclos'd.
>
> (ll. 1905–8)

Secondly, the play legitimates Cleopatra's relationship with Antony by appropriating conventional marriage terminology and gender roles. The adulterous love affair is referred to as a 'holy marriage'; Cleopatra is not the concubine but the 'wife-kindhearted'; Antony is her 'deare husband,' and their children 'our deare babes.' In this way the play also inadvertently annuls the marriage between Antony and Octavia and sets up the love relationship as the more authentic one of the two. This is not to say, of course, that the play condones Antony's treatment of his wife Octavia, for it does not. Antony is made to regret, among other things, his lack of respect for 'Thy wife Octavia and her tender babes' (l. 122). The translator, too, is sympathetic towards Octavia and critical of Antony. In the play's Argument (her own original composition) Mary Herbert states that Antony fell to 'his former loves, without any regarde of his vertuous wife Octavia, by whom nevertheles he had excellent children.' But the sympathetic references to Octavia do not convince us that Antony should go back to his legal wife; they are hardly enough to cancel any of the play's positive attitudes towards the principal characters. The sympathy towards Octavia, who in most sources had been presented as an example of female gentleness and fidelity, serves as a safeguard against any obvious rejection of the institutionalized marriage. It also enables a woman like Mary Herbert to publish the play without running the risk of appearing to endorse the abandonment of wives in favour of romantic lovers. The Octavia–Antony marriage which is being undermined in the play was the prevalent type among the aristocracy in England and exemplified, ironically, by the Countess's own to the Earl of Pembroke.

In addition to deploying conventional marriage and marital language, the play also deploys motherhood as a means of gathering support for Cleopatra. Unlike most other analogues, *Antonie* makes dramatic use of Cleopatra's children. Her parting from them is described in very moving terms:

> Farwell, my babes, farwell my heart is clos'd,
> With pittie and paine, my selfe with death enclos'd,
> My breath doth faile. Farwell for evermore,
> Your Sire and me you shall see never more.
> Farwell sweet care, farwell.

(ll. 1865–9)

This motherly quality further helps to erase the image of the seductress and to establish Cleopatra as a legitimate spouse: the mother of illegitimate children is, after all, still a mother. But while the play seems to capitalize on Cleopatra's role as a mother, it does not at the same time support conventional ideas on motherhood. It shows, on the contrary, that the lover's instinct is stronger than the mother's. This is clearly brought out in a stichomythia between Cleopatra and Charmion:

> *Ch.* Live for your sonnes. *Cl.* Nay for their father die.
> *Ch.* Hardhearted mother! *Cl.* Wife, kindhearted, I.
> *Ch.* Then will you them deprive of royall right?
> *Cl.* Do I deprive them? no, it's dest'nies might.
>
> (ll. 555–8)

In the conflict between maternal and romantic love, Cleopatra chooses the latter. Here and throughout the play she is made to affirm her identity as a faithful lover. Antony's love is to her 'More deare then Scepter, children, freedome, light' (l. 410). In the context of her idealism, her choice does not invite blame. Meanwhile, in the process of these dialectics, the play celebrates sexual love and undermines motherhood.

While conventionalizing Cleopatra with reference to the seductress figure, the play dismantles Antony's identity as the great warrior/hero. In his defeat, Antony is shown to be anything but the great warrior. His plaintive tone, his self-pity ('poore Antony,' he keeps saying to himself), his bitterness, and his jealousy reveal him to be very weak, or what by sixteenth-century conventional standards would be considered 'woman-like.' As several critics have pointed out, Cleopatra is the stronger one of the pair; she is less vacillating and more self-possessed. Yet, significantly, Antony's weakness seems to stem not from his position as an adulterous man (he is hardly blamed for loving Cleopatra) but from his dependence on martial glory as a source of strength. In revealing this weakness of Antony, the play throws into question traditional notions of masculinity and the basis of its strength, while at the same time it claims our sympathy for Antony the confused and self-deluded lover rather than Antony the debased man. It is interesting in this respect that Garnier's *Antonie* is the only play in the French and Italian neo-Senecan group which shows sympathy for, rather than disappointment in, the 'weak' behaviour of the fallen Antony.[19]

The play then does not condemn the lovers on moral grounds. Whatever blame is laid is bound up with matters of politics, precisely because the private identities of Antony and Cleopatra are not independent from their political identities. When Antony says that Cleopatra has 'triumphed' over him and that she alone shall 'command' him, his language keeps reminding us of the connection between the sexual and the political. Although this connection is not as interestingly explored in Garnier as it is, say, in Shakespeare (Garnier's characters are much less complex), the subject of realpolitik is very directly, although briefly, dealt with and so is the relation of political rulers to the people they govern.

Despite references to Destiny and Fortune, *Antonie* ultimately reveals that historical events are the products of power relations among rulers and that these relations are informed by sexual and political insecurities. Two prime examples of this are Cleopatra's decision to join Antony in battle lest once away he might return to Octavia, and Antony's fear during the battle that she was fleeing to side with Caesar. The play further explores the idea of fear as a determining element in the character of powerful rulers such as Antony and Caesar. Antony's main complaint in his fall, so he tells us, is not that he has lost his political power (empire), but that he has been defeated by a man whom he considers to be woman-like:

> A man, a woman both in might and minde,
> In Mars his schole who never lesson learn'd,
> Should me repulse, chase, overthrow, destroy,
> Me of such fame, bring to so low an ebbe?
>
> (ll. 1060–4)

In other words, Caesar has deprived Antony not only of his power as a ruler but also of his masculine virtue, for in Antony's mind manhood is directly related to martial performance. Apparently Antony associates his combat in war and politics with an opportunity to exhibit virility. Hence to be defeated by a stronger man is itself a kind of victory:

> Yet if to bring my glory to the ground,
> Fortune had made me overthrowne by one
> Of greater force, of better skill then I:
> One of those Captaines feared so of olde,
>
> ....
>
> The lesse her wrong, the lesse should be my woe:
> Nor she should paine, nor I complaine me so.
>
> (ll. 1080–93)

But Antony's comments about Caesar's weakness reflect his own insecurity and fear. His constant suspicion of and even

73

adamant belief in Cleopatra's betrayal, despite his friends' protestations to the contrary, is evidence of this. Furthermore, his pronouncement of Caesar's womanish weakness is a striking piece of irony, for it is he who has been displaying weak and 'unmanly' behaviour. Antony's conventional notions of masculinity cannot be taken at face value.

The ruler's struggle to maintain political power is the subject explored in relation to Caesar and his intended treatment of Antony. In the seventeenth chapter of his *The Prince*, Machiavelli states:

> Upon this a question arises: whether it be better to be loved than feared or feared than loved? It maybe answered that one should wish to be both, but, because it is difficult to unite them in one person, it is much safer to be feared than loved, when, of the two, either must be dispensed with.[20]

This is also Caesar's opinion in an argument he holds with Agrippa on the same subject in the fourth act of the play:

> *Caes.* Then to the end none . . .
> We must with bloud marke this our victory,
> For just example to all memorie
> Murther we must, until not one we leave,
> Which may hereafter us of rest berave.
> *Ag.*   Marke it with murthers? Who of that can like?
> *Caes.* Murthers must use, who doth assurance seeke.
> ....
> *Ag.*   What ease to him that feared is of all?
> *Caes.* Feared to be, and see his foes to fall.
> *Ag.*   Commonly feare doth brede and nourish hate.
> *Caes.* Hate without pow'r comes commonly too late.
> *Ag.*   A feared Prince hath oft his death desir'd.
> *Caes.* A Prince not fear'd hath oft his wrong conspir'd.
> *Ag.*   No guard so sure, no forte so strong doth prove,
> No such defence, as is the peoples love.
> (ll. 1495–1514)

Like Machiavelli's prince, Caesar places political expediency above consanguinity or loyalty to past alliance. 'Bloud and alliance nothing do prevaile,' says Antony referring to Caesar (l. 1010). According to Caesar, execution, not clemency, is the best treatment for his opponents. He must kill those who pose a threat to his power, hoping that the fear of such a severe punishment will act as a deterrent to active political opposition: 'For just example to all memorie' (l. 1498).

Antonie does not endorse or reject these political ideas. It simply shows the way they work. The play's position is less equivocal, however, with regard to the relationship between rulers and common people. The latter are shown to be unfortunately dependent on the former. This theme, present also in Shakespeare, is a very central one in Garnier. The latter is very clearly sympathetic towards the people who suffer as a result of shifts in power at the top ranks of the political hierarchy.

Although direct blame of Antony and Cleopatra specifically is avoided, criticism of those in power is expressed in several terms by the chorus and by powerless but creditable characters like Diomid, Philostratus, and Lucilius.

The chorus serves as a critical voice through its structural positioning in the play and its elegiac theme and tone. At the end of each act the choral passage forms a lamentation song on man's sufferings in general and on those of the Egyptians in particular. The juxtaposition of these passages forces the reader to consider the actors and the victims of the situation. Diomid, Philostratus, and Lucilius are more direct in their criticism. One of the main issues they address is the obligation of the rulers towards the people they govern. To what extent should a ruler's actions and personal life be guided by the interests of the governed? Diomid, Cleopatra's secretary, goes so far as to say that the ruler should sacrifice his/her individual concept of virtue and should deploy personal assets in the interest of the state. His recommendation for Cleopatra is not basically different from what Machiavelli advocated and Elizabeth I practised:

> Alas! It's our ill hap, for if hir teares
> She would convert into her loving charmes,
> To make a conquest of the conqueror,
> (As well she might, would she hir force imploie)
> She should us safetie from these ills procure,
> Hir crowne to hir, and to hir race assure.
>
> (ll. 735–40)

This course of action, which amounts to a form of prostitution, sounds unreasonably demanding on the 'pure' Cleopatra, until we are reminded (by Lucilius and Philostratus, especially) that it was she and Antony who created the disastrous situation in the first place. In this way the play exposes to criticism the queen's treatment of her affair with Antony as a purely domestic matter. Cleopatra's concern is how to be loyal to her lover and her children – not how to save the Egyptians from the disaster she has brought upon them. Philostratus, the philosopher, is in fact the only one who shows concern for the fate of the people. He addresses the chorus of Egyptians feelingly ('come you poore people') and from outside the palace walls comments on the situation created by those inside. He sees that the Egyptians are faced with captivity or death and hopes for the lesser of the two evils. The message is clear: the rulers have made a mess and the people must pay for it. This is the realist part of the play, which portrays governors according to the way they function in actuality. The idealist part shows the lovers attempting to abide by a form of behaviour which transcends reality.

The idealist and the realist aspects come into conflict. The play's sympathy for the woman (the lover) clashes with its criticism of Cleopatra the ruler. This conflict is not reconciled, or even clearly focused. But it is important that the play generates unorthodox questions with respect to sexuality and political power.

Was the translator aware of the play's oppositional potential? There is little evidence either way, but she cannot have been altogether unaware of the fact that she was introducing the English audience to a favourable view of Cleopatra. Daniel's play *Cleopatra*, written to accompany the Countess's, 'well-grac'd Anthony,' is based on the same favourable view.[21] The translator must also have been aware of Garnier's association with liberal ideas. Author of several neo-classical plays named after women and husband to an authoress, Garnier was very much preoccupied with the theme of political corruption and women's role as agents of justice. His heroines are far from the submissive wives of sixteenth-century conduct books. Porcie and Antigonie are admired for their fidelity to family and country, but such fidelity, though presented as pious, requires insubordination to tyrannical rule. His women are applauded for taking political action rather than condemned for interfering with men's politics. They are encouraged to be independent-minded, though apparently they are still expected to conform to society's rules regarding virtuous behaviour. But sexuality does not become a major criterion in their condemnation or approval. Although politically Garnier was not a radical, he was critical of authority. Looking mainly to the past for solutions, he sought reforms within the existing social and political structure. A republican sentiment runs through several of his plays, including *Antonie*.[22]

But consciously or not, Mary Herbert contributed to undermining certain dominant ideas in her culture. The woman's role as mother was considered one of the strongholds of the nuclear family and was elaborated in many guides.[23] The language of motherhood which the play deploys in the depiction of its heroine suggests that she is to be seen in this role. Yet Cleopatra rejects it to remain faithful to her lover – and she is not condemned. Indeed, sexual love receives a kind of glorification in the play as it becomes legitimized through marital language and at the same time idealized as worthy of sacrifice. In the sphere of politics, the play contributes to a demystification of the ruler's identity and power. Like many other Renaissance plays,[24] *Antonie* offers at least a glimpse into the actual mechanisms of state power. Perhaps Mary Herbert did not see this, but others around her may have. (One might call to mind Daniel's *Philotas* and its connection with the Essex affair.[25])

Mary Herbert left a useful legacy to women writers who came later. As a socially accepted type of a female intellectual model, she held the potential of being appropriated by conservative men to inhibit assertively creative women (as in the Denny–Wroth case described in chapter 4). But she could equally be appropriated by women writers in various constructive ways. Mary Wroth profited later from the metrical forms the Countess of Pembroke introduced in her translations, and Elizabeth Cary published a closet drama not unlike *Antonie*. As the first woman to publish a secular play in English,[26] Mary Herbert chose to translate the work of an author who might be called 'feminine' in his approach: Garnier presents female figures that women can identify with, and in his presentation he uses strategies which could be employed also by women writers. Moreover, the Countess's reputation among male authors as a competent versifier and serious supporter of literature helped to a recognition, even among limited literary circles, of women's artistic abilities. Daniel's remark in his dedication of *Cleopatra* that the Countess 'opened mens eyes' to women's talents is not merely praise; it is also a revealing statement which suggests that their eyes had been closed. When a woman writer achieves a certain reputation among her male colleagues she makes the atmosphere a little easier for other women who come after. In this respect Lady Pembroke's aristocratic status was very important because it lent validity to a model. A woman like Isabella Whitney who wrote more original poetry a couple of decades earlier could not have served as a model because she lacked high social standing.

ELIZABETH CARY: IDEALIZING AND VICTIMIZING THE TRANSGRESSOR

In literary dedications the name of Elizabeth Cary appeared next to that of Mary Herbert, her senior by nearly twenty-five years. Sir John Davies, for example, dedicates his *The Muses Sacrifice or Divine Meditations* 'To The Most Noble, and no lesse deservedly-renowned Ladyes, as well as Darlings, as Patronesses, of the Muses; Lucy, Countesse of Bedford; Mary, Countesse-Dowager of Pembroke; and, Elizabeth, Lady Cary, (Wife of Sr. Henry Cary:) Glories of Women.'[27] And there are good indications that Mary Herbert and Elizabeth Cary were, if not personally acquainted, at least familiar with each other's work. They shared an interest in closet-type drama, and they had common friends, such as Michael Drayton, who could serve as liaison for literary news and manuscript circulation. However, unlike the sister of Sir Philip Sidney, Elizabeth Cary grew up with few advantages. Before marriage, while still at her parental home, the intellectual atmosphere was far from congenial. Her father, intrigued by her intellectual gifts, let her use his library and occasionally tested her critical mind;[28] but her barely literate mother seems to have been especially strict and inimical to her daughter's learning. Lady Tanfield, we are told, forbade the servants to give young Elizabeth candles for reading and required her to kneel every time she spoke to her.[29]

Things did not apparently get much better for Elizabeth after her marriage at seventeen to Henry Cary, later First Viscount Falkland. During his first, long absence abroad, she had to live with a despotic mother-in-law, who was infuriated rather than impressed by Elizabeth's love for books.[30] Viewed against such a hostile environment, Lady Cary's literary and educational

The inscription on the statue reads:

Elizabeth (1585–1639)
Only child of TANFIELDS
Married 1600 Henry CARY
1st Viscount of Falkland — 1620

Figure 3.2 Elizabeth Cary, née Tanfield, wife of Henry Cary, Lord Deputy of Ireland, First Viscount Falkland, on the tomb of her parents in St Katherine's Chapel, Burford Parish Church.

accomplishments appear all the more striking. By the time she was eighteen she had taught herself several foreign languages, including French, Spanish, Italian, Latin, and Transylvanian; she had read a wide range of books (up to that time mainly poetry and history); had translated Seneca's epistles and Ortelius' geographical treatise *Le Mirroir du Monde* (which her uncle published for her in Amsterdam); and had written at least one original play, *The Tragedie of Mariam*, the first recorded drama by an Englishwoman.[31] Later on she wrote biographies of women saints and a *History of Edward II*. She also translated Du Perron's *Reply*, a lengthy religious treatise. All the while she was a very busy mother (always either pregnant or nursing a child) and a wife to a very demanding and authoritarian husband.

Cary's strong will and determination, qualities she apparently possessed from an early age, account perhaps for the fact that she was able to surmount obstacles in her immediate surroundings. But her achievements were made possible as well by changes in the wider social scene. In 1603, when King James ascended the throne, Elizabeth Cary was eighteen. By that time humanist influence had become pervasive, and women had begun to take greater liberties than theory allowed them. Also, more women were being educated, and a greater number of them had appeared as authors or translators of published works. I have already discussed the important role of Mary Herbert in this respect. It cannot be altogether coincidental that Cary's early drama, *Mariam*, is written in the French classical style established by the Countess of Pembroke and her followers. None the less, Lady Cary's life and literary work attest to the monumental difficulties an upper-class female writer was likely to encounter in the early seventeenth century.

In her personal life, Cary was a self-willed, independent-minded, and at times defiant woman, unlike Mary Herbert in these respects. Resisting pressures from her immediate environment, Cary usually managed to fulfil many of her wishes. When her mother denied her candles for reading, she bribed her servants to let her have some; when her tyrannical mother-in-law carried away the whole of her library, Elizabeth composed verses; much later, when her husband's attitude and career became obstacles to her religious activity and to her desire to join Catholicism, she converted secretly.[32] But as these and other facts recorded by her biographers show, Elizabeth Cary was at once a rebel and a conformist. Disinclined either to suppress her desires altogether or to claim for herself openly the right to act as an independent subject, she aimed to satisfy her desires by the clandestine manoeuvre rather than the open confrontation. She thus tried to resolve conflicts between her will and that of the people around her through a principle of accommodation: satisfying herself without offending others. The motto 'Be and Seem,' which she carved on her eldest daughter's wedding ring, expresses this principle: being true to oneself while avoiding 'what might have a show or suspicion of comeliness or unfitness.' In other words, one may be assertive, but may not appear to flout established rules of conduct, for by flouting them one offends and challenges those who make and support the rules.

This same theme of assertiveness and subjection, or rebellion and conformity, shows up in her two extant dramatic works, *Mariam* and *Edward II*, particularly in regard to the figure of the wife. That is, Cary's reluctance to support openly rebellious behaviour in her life carries over into her literary work. Her early play *Mariam* (1602–4) evidences the author's difficulty in endorsing fully the heroine's attempt to disengage herself from a criminal and jealous husband. In her later work, *Edward II* (1627), Cary seems considerably more assertive, although still cautious. Both works contain evidence of opposition to dominant ideologies.

Mariam

The *Tragedie of Mariam, The Faire Queene of Jewry* (written c.1604, published 1613) is based on the Herod story, interest in which had revived at the time Cary wrote her play. Josephus's *Wars* and *Antiquities*, in which the story appears, were translated by Thomas Lodge and published in 1602. As Cary most probably utilized Josephus's account,[33] it is worth noting a few things about it. Josephus's treatment of the situation in Palestine was very different from the account of other historians. Josephus had demythologized the figure of the heroic Herod and had analysed shrewdly both his foreign relations and domestic activities. The result was a first-century Palestine that bore a remarkable resemblance to early Stuart England. The society depicted by Josephus was, like the English, a patriarchal one with an absolute monarch in power. In both societies, nobility of birth was very highly prized, with a close connection between the monarch's power and the family squabbles of the aristocracy. Furthermore, the domestic situation described by Josephus, particularly the scene of scheming women, was strikingly similar to the one we know to have obtained in the society of early seventeenth-century England.

Cary's *Mariam* is one of a series of dramas dealing with the conflict between Herod and Mariam.[34] But it is apparently the only one, at least among the group printed or acted in Renaissance England, which dramatizes the conflict from Mariam's rather than from Herod's point of view;[35] it focuses on her inner conflict as a wife and shows the difficulty she experiences in subordinating herself to her husband. This choice of perspective in her drama probably reflects the author's own preoccupation with the husband/wife relationship in her own life at the time. (Cary was newly married or about to be married when she wrote *Mariam*.)

Before the time of the play's action, Herod had divorced his first wife, Doris, to marry the more beautiful and politically more useful Mariam. Subsequently, to secure his position, he had murdered Mariam's brother and grandfather, camouflaging the first crime as an accident and the second as an act of self-defence. These crimes had caused Mariam to turn cold towards him and her love to be replaced with scorn and rage. Herod's instructions to one of his servants, that Mariam should be killed as soon as his own death is announced, further fuelled Mariam's anger towards her husband. None the less, when news of Herod's death arrives, Mariam is the only one who does not feel altogether glad. The play opens with Mariam ('sola') pondering on her mixed feelings about the reported death of her husband:

> Now doe I finde by selfe Experience taught,
> One Object yeelds both griefe and joy:
> You wept indeed, when on his worth you thought,
> But joyd that slaughter did your Foe destroy.
> So at his death your Eyes true droppes did raine,
> Whom dead, you did not wish alive againe.
>
> (ll. 11–16)[36]

But when midway through the play the news of Herod's death proves to be only a rumour and Herod arrives in Palestine,

Mariam's suppressed feelings of fear, anger, and resentment surface again. She cannot trust what Herod might do if she refuses to receive him joyfully. At the same time she resents having to smooth over the situation by compromising her conscience. Scorning to use deceit as a way out ('I cannot frame disguise,' l. 1407), she decides to make her disposition clear to him – and thus also to assert her independence – by denying him his sexual claim on her as his wife: 'I will not to his love be reconcilde,/ With solemne vowes I have forsworne his Bed' (ll. 1135–6). Refusing to understand the real cause of his wife's discontent, Herod misinterprets her attitude and charges her with inconstancy. Egged on by his scheming sister Salome, he gives orders for his wife's death. 'The stately Mariam' receives the sentence with Roman-like dignity.

Cary's Mariam is quite an assertive woman. In her, Cary gives us an example of wifely insubordination in the context of seventeenth-century patriarchal society, which identified woman, legally and socially, as her husband's dependant. Unlike Griselda, the contemporary model of feminine patience and wifely subservience, and like Cary herself in later life, Mariam refuses to sacrifice her idealism in favour of wifely duty. There is some ambiguity with respect to the ultimate causes of her death, but the play as a whole makes clear that Mariam ultimately dies primarily because she insists on remaining, in Belsey's phrase, 'a unified, autonomous subject.'[37]

Mariam refuses to act according to prescribed social norms. She opposes her husband's criminal tactics and attempts to establish a perspective from which she can speak as a person who has a conscience of her own to answer to. In the character of Mariam, then, the play provides us with an example of wifely insubordination and hence opposition to the Griselda model. Mariam does not appear to regard the marriage bond as a *raison d'être*; in fact, using her own criteria of decent human conduct, she sets herself up as a judge of her husband's actions. More generally, through Mariam the play queries the validity of a universal standard on wifely behaviour and simultaneously challenges the assumption behind this standard – that man is necessarily woman's moral superior. Ultimately, the play undermines many of the assumptions on which Cary's society based its definition of a wife.

But does Cary endorse Mariam's rebellious behaviour? What is the author's attitude *vis-à-vis* her heroine and the other female characters who hustle and bustle throughout the play? The answer is not straightforward. Cary's own attitude is ambivalent but also revealing of the tension between internalized cultural restrictions and individual desire.

Several things about Mariam indicate that the author labours to legitimate her heroine's character and position. One of these things is the idealization Mariam undergoes. This idealization can be more clearly seen when we compare Cary's Mariam with the Mariam in Josephus, its likely source. The two are very much alike: beautiful, witty, chaste, noble of birth. But Cary refines her portrait by excluding overtly sexual or other conventionally exceptionable traits. Josephus's Mariam is contentious, forward, and scheming, using 'prettie presents and feminine flatteries' to elicit secret information from Sohemus, Herod's servant.[38] Cary gets rid of such traits, which might make Mariam appear frivolously insubordinate. Above all, Cary endows her heroine with marital chastity and moral stature. Mariam does not love another man; not only that, but she categorically rejects adultery as an option:

But yet too chast a Scholler was my hart,
To learne to love another then my Lord:
To leave his Love, my lessons former part,
I quickly learn'd, the other I abhord.

(ll. 29–32)

Cary also idealizes her heroine by placing her in contrast to other assertive or rebellious women, like Salome and Cleopatra, making it quite clear that Mariam is different from them. (Cleopatra does not actually figure in the play but she is alluded to several times.) The Countess of Pembroke had, as we have seen, recently translated and published a flattering version of a sexually modest and wifely Cleopatra. Cary does not rely on such a version. Working through contrast rather than similarity, she deploys an older and more denigrating image of the Egyptian queen to lend conventional support to her heroine. Mariam proudly declares:

Not to be Emprise of aspiring Rome,
Would Mariam like to Cleopatra live:
With purest body will I presse my Toome,
And wish no favours Anthony could give.

(ll. 204–7)

The implication here is that Cleopatra is morally 'impure' because she exchanges sexual for political favours. By contrast, Mariam is 'pure' because she places principle above expediency. Although the above and other statements made by Mariam must be taken with caution and not be automatically identified with the author, they do appear to strengthen the heroine's character in conventional terms: Mariam is a morally upright and honest woman. Deception, or improper use of sexuality, is clearly ruled out by her as a means of attaining her goals:

I know I could inchaine him with a smile:
And lead him captive with a gentle word,
I scorne my looke should ever man beguile,
Or other speech, then meaning to afford.

(ll. 1166–9)

In the play itself, Mariam is placed in contrast to Salome, the villainess, spiritual sister of Edmund and Vittoria. Having gone through one husband and wishing to get rid of her present one (Constabarus) to marry a third (Silleus), Salome is not willing to bow to social rules, or even laws, that contradict her desires. Unlike Mariam, she flouts conventional morality because she has no use for it. She knows the terms by which society judges her actions, and at times she appears to accept them. But she is not interested in obtaining people's good opinion; she is after more substantial gains towards which she will use any means. The following passage is from a soliloquy:

But shame is gone, and honour wipt away,
And Impudencie on my forehead sits:
She bids me worke my will without delay,
And for my will I will imploy my wits.

(ll. 303–6)

By placing Mariam in contrast to women like Salome and Cleopatra, Cary imparts credibility and respectability to her heroine.

Besides establishing Mariam as a conventionally respectable woman, the author also musters support for the conflict she experiences. Cary validates Mariam's dilemma by giving her a strong cause. As the situation is set up, with Mariam's knowledge of her husband's crimes, Mariam would have to be either imbecile or monstrous to go on loving a man who has murdered her kin. Furthermore, Cary legitimates Mariam's position by undermining that of Herod. The play shows that even his love, which could be valued as a redeeming feature, is of the selfish, narcissistic type. Herod is a dangerously possessive man. His command that Mariam should be killed after his death is discovered early in the play and looms heavily in Mariam's as well as the reader's mind. Herod's love develops out of his complacency with his position in the world.[39] Through both fair and foul means he has possessed anything he has wanted, including Mariam. Hence to continue to possess Mariam is to reaffirm his own abilities and desires. He does not love Mariam for *her* but for *himself*. His self-complacency and sense of control over others does not allow him to think that Mariam might not want to be loved in his terms. 'Mariamne is a part of Herod only in the mind of Herod. She does not acquiesce in his identification.'[40]

Yet there is also evidence which suggests the author's reluctance to endorse fully her heroine's outspoken rebelliousness. Cary wants her heroine to obey conventional rules of feminine behaviour, but she also wants her to have an independent mind. The latter, though appropriate for the French classical style of the play, is fundamentally incompatible with the sixteenth-century notion of the married woman as the husband's complete dependant.[41] The result is contradiction, uneasiness, and tension. Mariam is outspoken, self-confident, and self-assured, but it is for these qualities that she is censured by various characters in the play. Sohemus, Herod's servant, has jeopardized his own life to spare Mariam's, for, in his self-deprecating opinion, 'Ten such [as himself] were better dead then she destroi'd' (l. 1207). Yet even he admits to a fault in Mariam, by way of paying her a compliment: 'Unbridled speech is Mariams worst disgrace' (l. 1186). Immediately following Sohemus's praise, the chorus ('a Companie of Jews') indirectly criticizes Mariam when it comments on women who fail to submit body and mind to their marriage partners:

When to their Husbands they themselves doe bind,
Doe they not wholy give themselves away?
Or give they but their body not their mind,
Reserving that though best, for others pray?
   No sure, their thoughts no more can be their owne,
   And therefore should to none but one be knowne.
                      (ll. 1237–42)

Further on, the chorus directly censures Mariam's attitude:

Had Mariam scorn'd to leave a due unpaide,
Shee would to Herod then have paid her love:
And not have bene by sullen passion swaide
To fixe her thoughts all injurie above
   Is vertuous pride. Had Mariam thus bene prov'd,
   Long famous life to her had bene allowd.
                      (ll. 1934–9)

Here and elsewhere, Mariam is criticized for speaking her mind openly and for possessing the wrong kind of pride (identified by the chorus as 'sullen passion'). Yet these and similar passages come into contradiction with the overall implications of the play's actions. As Belsey aptly remarks, 'the play as a whole makes clear that what brings about Mariam's death is not her openness with other people but her outspoken defiance of Herod himself. . . . Mariam is in danger because she speaks her thoughts to Herod.'[42]

The play, then, is not transparent but ambiguous about the heroine's behaviour. The text's ambiguity seems to be a sign of the author's ambivalence about accommodating cultural ideas on the woman's role. It is also a sign of her difficulty in accepting the play's own theoretical implications. Cary quite clearly shows that she is aware of the uneven distribution of power between men and women in the society she portrays. There is no better evidence of her awareness than the statements she puts in the mouth of Salome about divorce and the double standard:

He loves, I love; what then can be the cause,
Keepes me for being the Arabians wife?
It is the principles of Moses lawes,
For Con[s]tabarus still remaines in life,
If he to me did beare as Earnest hate,

As I to him, for him there were an ease,
A separating bill might free his fate:
From such a yoke that did so much displease.
Why should such priviledge to man be given?
Or given to them, why bard from women then?
Are men then we in greater grace with Heaven?
Or cannot women hate as well as men?
Ile be the custome-breaker: and beginne
To shew my Sexe the way to freedomes doore.
(ll. 307–20)

But there is little doubt that, at least on the conscious level,[43] Cary opposes such views in the play. Constabarus, a creditable and sympathetic, if ineffectual character seems to express the author's position when he asks:

Are Hebrew women now transform'd to men?
Why do you not as well our battels fight,
And weare our armour? suffer this, and then
Let all the world be topsie turved quite.
(ll. 435–8)

Betty Travitsky correctly notes that Cary had internalized patriarchal attitudes and constructs of women.[44] Probably this internalization prevented Cary from endorsing Salome's views and possibly recognizing the full extent of women's plight under patriarchy. We, from a twentieth-century point of view, can see that the play's women are victims of a society which denies them their rights and pits one against the other: Doris against Mariam, Alexandra against both (for different reasons), and Salome against more or less anyone who stands in her way. But it is not at all clear that the author sees the women of her play in the same light. She is sympathetic towards her male characters. Constabarus and Pheroras are victims of Herod's tyrannical rule as well as of women's schemes, yet taking Herod's position as given, they throw the blame for what befalls them on the women. Of course part of the problem here is inherent in the story Cary has chosen to dramatize. Because he is a tyrant, Herod strikes indiscriminately at both men and women if they pose a threat to his power or challenge his authority. Both sexes become his victims in some way. Thus the disadvantageous position of the women in the play is not sufficiently distinguished from that of the men. Herod's role as tyrant obscures interesting distinctions.

Yet one wonders how much of the ambiguity referred to above is due to the author's own conflicting attitudes towards her culture's ideology and how much it is actually the result of the author's precarious and delicate position as the first woman to write a drama, although not for stage production. In the period we are speaking of, how does a woman of Cary's class and upbringing come forward to write a drama and be firm in expressing her views? Indeed, whatever we finally say about the play, we must keep in mind that *Mariam* was suppressed when it was finally published (approximately ten years from the time of its composition). Unfortunately we know almost nothing about the circumstances of this incident, except for the daughter's elliptic remark that the play was printed without her mother's knowledge.[45] But there is little doubt that the play had offended some of the conservative members of Cary's family, including her own husband, who was then on his way to becoming Knight of the Bedchamber in the court of James I. It is therefore quite possible, indeed probable, that some of the faltering we sense in the play might be related to the author's attempt to contain what might otherwise offend. Cary may be applying here the 'Be and Seem' principle which she used in her life as a means of reconciling personal assertion and cultural prohibitions. We recognize this principle in the chorus's advice on wifely conduct:

> Tis not enough for one that is a wife
>> To keepe her spotles from an act of ill:
>> But from suspition she should free her life.
>>> (ll. 1219–21)

And we find an interesting application of it in the opening of the play as the heroine enters the scene with an apology:

> How oft have I with *publike voyce* runne on?
> To censure Romes last Hero [Caesar?] for deceit:
> Because he wept when Pompeis life was gone,
> Yet when he liv'd, hee thought his Name too great.
> But now I doe recant, and Roman Lord
> Excuse too rash a judgement in a woman:
> *My Sexe pleads pardon, pardon then afford,*
> Mistaking is with us, but too too common.
>> (ll. 3–10; emphasis added)

89

This could very well serve as Cary's own apology for assuming the 'publike voyce' of a dramatist. Much of her reservation and unease, therefore, can be read as an attempt on her part to remain *inoffensively* assertive. This also explains her reluctance to expose her works to public view. Sir John Davies's comment that Cary was in the habit of giving her works 'both Birth and Grave' is very revealing, and so is her daughter's reference to the surreptitious publication of *Mariam*.

Furthermore, there is at least one scene in the play which should warn us to avoid oversimplified statements on Cary's position in relation to radical ideas. This is Act IV, scene 8. Alone in the scene, Mariam muses on the recent course of events; and although she chastises herself for not possessing enough humility, along with chastity, she is overall quite satisfied with herself, especially with her moral innocence: 'tis my joy,/That I was ever innocent, though sower' (ll. 1841–2). But Mariam's perception of herself, of her morality, and of her relation to other women is placed under scrutiny. Just as she announces, 'My Soule is free from adversaries power' (l. 1844), Doris, her greatest adversary, walks in and accuses her of adultery:

> Your soule is blacke and spotted, full of sinne:
> You in adultry liv'd nine yeare together.
>
> (ll. 1850–1)

Mariam, who has always been proud of her sexual purity, is taken aback and defends herself by appealing to the Mosaic law on divorce:

> Was that adultry: did not Moses say,
> That he that being matcht did deadly hate:
> Might by permission put his wife away,
> And take a more belov'd to be his mate?
>
> (ll. 1861–4)

Yet Doris seems to win the case with her logic:

> What did he hate me for: for simple truth?
> For bringing beautious babes for love to him:
> For riches: noble birth, or tender youth,
> Or for no staine did Doris honour dim?
>
> (ll. 1865–8)

Less eloquently, perhaps, Doris here challenges the double standard of Mosaic law that Salome had challenged earlier in the play. But the significant difference is that in this scene Cary appears to be on Doris's side. She puts sensible arguments in this woman's mouth and hints at the idea that Mariam may not be so very innocent after all. The scene I have just referred to queries legal definitions of adultery and the text threatens to break into a validated castigation of the double standard. Cary is openly sympathetic to Doris, whom she presents as a victim of patriarchal laws. Doris is allowed to express her feelings of anger and revenge (which are perhaps of necessity misdirected at Mariam?) without judgement or condemnation. In fact these feelings serve to remind us of the wrongs done to her and invite our sympathy.

Edward II

Some twenty-five years after her first published play, *Mariam*, and during a solitary confinement that followed her secret conversion to Catholicism in 1626, Cary also wrote a *History of King Edward II*, which appears to be an unfinished play or a biography influenced by drama.[46] The work survives in two versions, both printed in 1680 by different printers. The longer one of the two, published in a folio volume,[47] seems to be closer to the form of a play. It contains several speeches and is written predominantly in blank verse; it is also clearer, more coherent, and less sentimental in tone. The shorter version, which came out in a small octavo book, appears to be a condensed account of the longer piece.[48] Because it was found among Lord Falkland's papers, *Edward II* had been attributed to him by the 1680 printers and subsequently by the editors of an eighteenth-century miscellany that reprinted the short version. This attribution went unchallenged until relatively recently when Donald Stauffer proved it to be Lady Cary's composition.[49]

As in the case of *Mariam*, the author's choice of subject matter for a literary work is suggestive of her concerns. *Edward II* deals as much with the relationship between the king and the queen as with that between the king and his subjects. Elizabeth Cary is once more attracted to a story which focuses on the relationship between the two genders and which treats a situation close to home. In her version of Edward II's life she shows familiarity with a long line of writers who treated the same subject before her.[50] Highly eclectic in her use of available material, she seems to have relied primarily on Grafton and to a lesser extent on Marlowe, although her sources cannot be easily identified.[51] From Marlowe she has apparently borrowed the incident of the king being shaved in cold puddle water, Gaveston's Italian identity, and Edward's neglect of and callous behaviour towards Queen Isabel.[52] But she has not lifted or borrowed material on a large scale from any particular author. This suggests that Cary felt the need to write her own original story, not merely to retell one already told. Apparently she was not satisfied with the way the subject had been dealt with. Indeed she lets us know as much in her 'Preface to the Reader' when she refers to the 'dull character of our Historians,' who write by inference and try to please 'Time' rather than 'Truth.' Although, as I discuss later, her own statement about Truth needs to be taken with caution, she evidently felt that the story had not been told quite right. Her dissatisfaction seems to have been greater with the treatment the queen had received, for it is in this respect that her account differs most from the versions of her predecessors. Her portrait of Edward is not very different from Marlowe's. Nor does she have anything particularly new to say about absolute monarchy as a governing system; her criticism seems specifically aimed at Edward for using his power arbitrarily and setting a bad example for his subjects.[53]

But the case is very different with respect to Queen Isabel. Unlike Marlowe and others who offer a perfunctory sketch of the queen and maintain an ambivalent attitude towards her, Elizabeth Cary treats Isabel with a great deal of sympathy, provides justification for her adultery, and labours to develop her into a consistent character.[54] What becomes evident in the process is Lady Cary's attempt to express herself without openly violating cultural norms or personal convictions regarding proper conduct in general and feminine conduct in particular.

The defence of Queen Isabel is attempted chiefly through a process of victimization. Almost throughout the work, Isabel is shown to be a woman and a wife trapped in a situation to whose making she has not contributed and out of which she tries to escape. Her marriage to Edward has been a stopgap solution to the king's homosexual passion: 'the interest of a wife was thought the most hopeful inducement to reclaim these loose affections' that had gone to Gaveston (p. 18).[55] As a wife – 'in name a Wife, in truth a Hand-maid' (p. 52) – she is forced to play the standby role accorded her by her husband and his minions. Even her trip to France is originally engineered by Spencer, who wishes 'to pare her nails before she scratch'd him' (p. 87), with the consent of her husband who 'could be contented well to spare her whose eyes did look too far into his pleasures' (p. 88). This kind of presentation has the effect of legitimating many of Isabel's actions. Her flight to France becomes not a traitorous act but an attempt to escape oppression at home.

The process of victimization is also deployed in what perhaps constitutes the most daring aspect of the author's task – her justification of Isabel's adultery. This is apparent from the queen's first full appearance, one third into the work:

> Love and Jealousie, that equally possess the Queen, being intermixed with a stronger desire of Revenge, spurs her on to hasten on this Journey [to France]. She saw the King a stranger to her bed, and revelling in the wanton embraces of his stoln pleasures, without a glance on her deserving Beauty. This contempt had begot a like change in her, though in a more modest nature, her youthful Affections wanting a fit subject to work on, and being debarr'd of that warmth that should have still preserv'd their temper, she cast her wandering eye upon the gallant Mortimer, a piece of masculine Bravery without exception.
>
> (p. 89)

With psychological insight, the author here renders Edward responsible for his wife's infidelity. Unlike previous writers, Cary recognizes the affective and sexual needs of Isabel as a young woman ('her youthful Affections wanting a fit subject to work on') and treats Edward's homosexuality as a form of adultery. Through his behaviour, Edward is shown to be the first to invalidate the marriage agreement. Hence the author justifies Isabel's lack of marital chastity and implicitly also opposes the role of the patient Griselda prescribed by her culture in similar situations.

But adultery was a serious offence when committed by a woman and Lady Cary was no doubt aware of her culture's prejudice on this matter. If she wanted to engage the reader's sympathy for the queen, she had to be very careful.[56] Besides casting her heroine as a victim, Cary uses a number of other tactics that seem to work in favour of the queen's character. Elements of time and space seem deployed to control the reader's response to Isabel's adulterous actions. Accordingly, the queen's appearance in the history is strategically delayed until Edward's abusiveness has been sufficiently – and emphatically – exposed. Her affair with Mortimer is given minimal description, while he is made to appear more like a companion to her griefs (p. 104) than a sexual partner. Conveniently, he is set aside and only occasionally referred to until the last few scenes, despite the fact that he accompanies the queen to France. Traditional notions of feminine sexual conduct are likewise appropriated to render the queen more acceptable and sympathetic. Thus Isabel's sexual behaviour is of 'a more modest nature' than her husband's (p. 89), and her speech to her brother is characterized by 'a sweetly-becoming modestie' (p. 96). The 'showre of Chrystal tears' she sheds (p. 97) is pitiable and proper for a woman's supposed soft nature.

Furthermore, the author strengthens the queen's position in the history by endowing her with a caring nature and a motherly instinct. Her character, unlike her husband's, is fortified with a care for the oppressed: "tis not I alone unjustly suffer,' she pleads, 'my tears speak those of a distressed Kingdom, which, long time glorious, now is almost ruin'd' (p. 96). Although structurally the eldest son's presence is needed so that he can claim the throne when his mother's party returns from France, the specific reference to her son, especially in the short version, suggests more than is necessary for the structure of the plot: 'Her eldest Son, her dearest comfort, and the chief spring that must set all these wheels a going, she leaves not behind, but makes him the Companion of her Travels' (octavo, p. 38). Additionally, the queen is credited with the good opinion and support of respectable people. Robert of Artois, a 'steady States-man, not led by Complement, or feign'd professions,' speaks of the queen's 'deeds of Goodness' (pp. 105, 106); and the Earl of Heinault, a man of 'an honest Heart and grave Experience,' decides to join his brother, Sir John, in defending 'a Queen that justly merits Love and Pity' (p. 112). Even Edward's own feelings regarding his wife's infidelity appear to be deployed in her favour: 'he thinks the breach of Wedlock a foul trespass; but to contemn her he so much had wronged, deserv'd as much as they could lay upon him' (p. 95).[57] Through these strategies, then, the author manages to pre-empt criticism of the queen as adultress and disloyal subject.

In previous treatments of Edward's life, the queen's character had been denigrated by attributing to her cruelty, which I shall discuss shortly, and hypocrisy. In Elizabeth Cary's portrayal of Isabel, hypocrisy is relatively absent. There are two obvious allusions to the queen's hypocritical behaviour. One is shortly before her flight to France when 'She courts her Adversary [Spencer] with all the shews of perfect reconcilement,' pretending to be 'well pleased, and glad to stay at home' (p. 90). The other occurs when she is about to escape from France: having been deceived by the French Council, she quits the French court 'in shew contented' (p. 108) and 'praiseth Spencer, as if 'twere he alone had wrought her Welfare' (p. 107). As may be discerned, however, this type of hypocrisy is presented as a valuable skill, one which Isabel learns of necessity and which finally saves her life.[58] It is not a blemish but an admirable quality allied to cunning and envied even by the cleverest politician. Rather than hold it against the queen, Cary uses it to poke fun at Spencer who, for all his ingenuity, is outwitted by a woman more than once: '[his] Craft and Care . . . here fell apparent short of all Discretion, to be thus over-reach'd by one weak Woman' (p. 92); 'Thus Womens Wit sometimes can cozen Statesmen' (p. 109). In this way, the author cleverly turns what other writers had set up as vice into a positive attribute of the queen's character.

The defence of the queen lapses at one point and discloses Cary's difficulty in handling her heroine. As we have seen, Isabel is not criticized for assuming political power. Although the sudden possession of power in the end turns her into a revengeful woman, she is overall portrayed as an intelligent and skilful politician whose manoeuvres in the battle with the Spencers win her a victory. (With one summons she manages to bring Arundel, Spencer, and the city of Bristol into her possession.) But she is severely criticized for the cruel treatment of her fallen adversaries, particularly and especially of Spencer:

While She thus passeth on with a kinde of insulting Tyranny, far short of the belief of her former Vertue and Goodness, she makes this poor unhappy man attend her Progress, not as the antient Romans did their vanquish'd Prisoners, for ostentation, to increase their Triumph; but merely for Revenge, Despite, and private Rancour. . . . Certainly this man was infinitely vicious, and deserv'd as much as could be laid upon him, for those many great and insolent Oppressions, acted with Injustice, Cruel[t]y, and Blood; yet it had been much more to the Queens Honour, if she had given him a quicker Death, and a more honourable Tryal, free from these opprobrious and barbarous Disgraces, which savour'd more of a savage, tyrannical disposition, than a judgment fit to command, or sway the Sword of Justice.

(pp. 128–9)

This is severe condemnation and not the only one of its kind. But it does not mark a change in the author's overall attitude toward her heroine. As the phrasing in the passage just quoted might suggest ('far short of the belief of her former Vertue and Goodness'), Cary strives to make Isabel as consistent a character as possible. This pause in the queen's defence seems rather a manifestation of the author's difficulty in reconciling the material she inherited from her sources, on the one hand, with her personal convictions and cultural values on the other. In order to better understand Elizabeth Cary's attitude toward cruelty, it would be useful to pay attention to other instances of it in the work. Early in the history, the beheading of Lancaster and twenty-two other nobles in 'a bloody Massacre' is the act of the 'cruel Tyrant,' Edward (p. 73). Bishop Stapleton's death is 'inhumane and barbarous' at the hands of the 'enraged multitude; who neither respecting the Gravity of his Years, or the Dignity of his Profession, strike off his Head, without either Arraignment, Tryal, or Condemnation' (p. 121). Old Spencer is likewise treated 'not with pity, which befits a Prisoner, but with insulting joy, and base derision' (p. 128).

The above passages indicate, among other things, that the author holds strong views on the subject of cruelty and by extension suggest the difficulties which she may have encountered in dealing with this aspect of her heroine's character. The historical sources had more or less established the major events of the story. Even Marlowe, who probably gives Isabel the most favourable treatment among male writers, shows her at the end to be a hypocritical and cruel woman. Cary could appropriate hypocrisy and turn it into an advantage, as we have seen. But cruelty was too strong a blemish. Silence on the matter was therefore neither possible nor desirable, since it would have left the queen exposed at the most critical point. A justification of cruelty, on the other hand, would have contradicted the author's own principles about proper Christian behaviour. Indeed, implied in the author's criticism of cruelty is a notion of justice that combines Christian ethics with a sense of fairness in the exercise of power. According to this notion, revenge in the form of cruelty toward a powerless subject (in this case a fallen adversary) is both unfair and unchristian:

> It is assuredly . . . an argument of a Villanous Disposition, and a Devilish Nature, to tyrannize and abuse those wretched ruines which are under the Mercy of the Law, whose Severity is bitter enough without aggravation. . . . In Christian Piety, which is the Day-star that should direct and guide all humane Actions, the heart should be as free from all that's cruel, as being too remiss in point of Justice.
>
> (p. 129)

In her own life too Elizabeth Cary abided by these principles. Her biographers tell us that treating the offender with kindness was one of her life-long convictions.[59] The spectacle of cruelty itself was a violation of her ideas about comeliness and fitness. Furthermore, in the author's culture, cruelty was a characteristically unfeminine vice. The connection between cruelty and femininity is apparent even in the language that the author uses: 'The queen's act is far unworthy of the Nobility of her Sex and Virtue' (octavo, p. 59). Noticeably, there is no apology for Mortimer's cruelty. The author thus chose what seems like a twist: she maintained the defence of the queen but condemned her cruelty.

Departing once more from her predecessors, Cary confines Isabel's cruelty mainly to the case of Spencer. With the interval just discussed, she again takes up the defence of the relative innocence of her heroine until the crucial last part – Edward's death. Significantly, the queen is shown to disapprove of the plans to murder the king: 'The Queen, whose heart was yet believed innocent of such foul Murther, is, or at least seems, highly discontented' (p. 151). This is made especially poignant and dramatic in the final speeches she exchanges with Mortimer in which she is made to declare: 'ne're can my heart consent to kill my Husband' (p. 152). The killing of Edward is presented as being almost entirely Mortimer's doing. When Mortimer suggests the idea, she tries to dissuade him. She finally succumbs to his pressure, but on condition that she will be spared the spectacle and 'be not made partaker, or privy to the time, the means, the manner' (p. 154).

It is difficult to say how the dramatic situation would have ended had it been put in the final form of a play, but as it is, the history lingers on after Edward's death, which is followed by a long moralizing on how much he deserved his punishment. Both Edward and Richard II are mentioned as examples of oppressive kings who abused their right to kingship and who died providentially: 'But his [Edward's] Doom was registred by that inscrutable Providence of Heaven who, with the self-same Sentence, punish'd both him, and Richard the Second, his great Grandchild, who were guilty of the same Offences' (octavo, p. 74). In the folio volume there is a more severe criticism of the subjects who betray the king and of their decision to depose and murder him. But even here the final responsibility for Edward's misfortune is made to fall on himself: 'had he not indeed been a Traytor to himself, they could not all have wronged him' (p. 160). Clearly, then, the author makes Edward's end a providential piece of work, and while she implicates Mortimer she exonerates the queen. The deaths of Mortimer and Isabel do not fall within the same chronological range, but significantly, only Mortimer is reported to have paid for his actions by death. The queen, 'who was guilty but in circumstance,' experienced only the pangs of conscience.

When we compare *The History of Edward II* with *Mariam*, we notice that the later work displays an assertiveness that seems to be lacking in the earlier one. 'The Author's Preface to the Reader,' dated and prefixed to the folio volume of *Edward II*, provides the most direct evidence of Elizabeth Cary's ability to assert herself as a writer. The latter part of this preface is worth quoting:

I have not herein followed the dull Character of our
Historians, nor amplified more than they infer, by Circumstance. I strive to please the Truth, not Time; nor fear I
Censure, since at the worst, 'twas one Month mis-spended;
which cannot promise ought in right Perfection.

If so you hap to view it, tax not my Errours; I my self
confess them.

(A2v)

What is interesting in this Preface is that there is no apology for
the author's sex or, more importantly, for the subject taken up.
On the contrary, there is a boldness, not unlike that which we
find in her address to the reader in the translation of *The Reply
of the Most Illustrious Cardinall of Perron*, published three years
later:

Reader Thou shalt heere receive a Translation wel intended. . . . I desire to have noe more guest at of me, but
that I am a Catholique, and a Woman: the first serves for
mine honor, and the second, for my excuse, since if the
worke be but meanely done, it is noe wonder, for my Sexe
can raise noe great expectation of anie thing that shall come
from me: yet were it a great follie in me, if I would expose
to the view of the world, a worke of this kinde, except I
judged it, to want nothing fitt, for a Translation. Therefore
I will confesse, I thinke it well done, and so had I confest
sufficientlie in printing it.[60]

A boldness and a self-confidence characterize both addresses to
the reader. In the address of the *Reply* there is of course the
conventional humility. But it is shown to be no more than
a worn-out topos, for in the next sentence the author turns
around and repudiates the excuse. She confidently asserts that
she finds the work very well done and that, woman or not,
she would not have published it unless she thought it met
her standards of publishable quality. In both addresses, the
reader's attention is diverted from the controversial subject itself
– Catholicism in the one and criticism of absolute rule coupled
with justification of adultery in the other – to the quality of the
work. The focus is shifted to perfectability, the execution of the
ideas. Most importantly, in both addresses the author presents
her task as telling the 'Truth' or 'informing [the reader] aright.'

This is an appropriation of the notion of absolute truth, the one truth which everyone has the right, indeed the obligation, to tell. This notion, which is found in much religious writing of the period and which Cary probably acquired from her long experience with religious materials, becomes in fact a very effective strategy which allows the author to tell the story from her perspective. In *Mariam* she had expressed several traditional notions of womanhood. Her heroine, idealized according to the standards of sixteenth-century culture, had to suffer patiently under a tyrannical husband and remain free from moral blemish: Mariam was not allowed to find recourse in adultery. In *Edward II* Cary still voices traditional notions of female conduct, but here these notions are deployed as writing strategies. As I have argued, this becomes especially apparent when it is viewed in conjunction with the author's appropriation of structural elements, such as space and time. If indeed the author had an audience in mind, she could not have afforded to alienate her readers. Expressing the ideas was as important as gaining acceptance of them.

The tone of voice in *Edward II* also marks a change from that in *Mariam*. This is particularly apparent in the narrative portions of the history, where Cary sounds what we today would call argumentative and moralizing. Here is an example:

> But what could be expected, when to satisfie his own unjust Passions, he had consented to the Oppressions of his Subjects, tyranniz'd over the Nobility, abus'd his Wedlock, and lost all fatherly care of the Kingdom, and that Issue that was to succeed him. Certainly it is no less honourable than proper, for the Majesty and Greatness of a King, to have that same free and full use of his Affection and Favour, that each particular Man hath in his oeconomic government; yet as his Calling is the greatest, such should be his care, to square them always out by those Sacred Rules of Equity and Justice.
>
> (octavo, p. 62)

Passages of this sort are not rare. In *Mariam* Cary had used didactic lines for the chorus, which served to express conventional wisdom on wifely conduct. But in *Edward II* this didacticism develops into a sophisticated argumentative technique. In the later work the appropriation of ideas and events seems to be a rhetorical strategy to gain her audience's acceptance rather than an attempt to protect the male reader from being offended. Furthermore, the moralizing is frequently expressed in religious terms. This I have already partly shown in my discussion of Cary's attitude towards cruelty. Here I will provide one more instance, which concerns the author's interpretation of Spencer's failure to prevent the escape of the queen and her party: 'But when the glorious power of Heaven is pleased to punish Man for his transgression, he takes away the sense and proper power by which he should foresee and stop his danger' (p. 92).

Given the events that intervened between the composition of her two dramas, we could say that this change in tone is at least partly the result of Elizabeth Cary's long and active struggle for her religious faith. Her experience, which included the reading, writing, and translating of religious material, apparently influenced her style and helped her to become more assertive. The translation of Du Perron's *Reply* in particular was an exercise not only in theological argument but also in polemical tactics, as it is a long and vigorous defence of Catholicism against Protestant charges. Religious dissidence, it seems, encouraged Cary's own critical propensity by teaching her how to challenge officially imposed beliefs.

Lady Herbert and Lady Cary, two aristocrats and near contemporaries, emerge as different personalities who share the common goal of trying to find room for self-expression within the confines of their culture and their class. Herbert is quiet, outwardly conventional. She works from backstage, translating serious books and directing with her influence the literary activity of men who will voluntarily comply with her wishes. Cary is a self-contained rebel. However much she wants to please others, she will not, or not always, sacrifice her own wishes. She uses her literary acquaintances but writes her own books in a hostile and authoritarian family environment. Both of them establish a female perspective, sympathizing with women and showing that the various roles into which they are cast – lovers, queens, wives, mothers – are incompatible. They resist denigrating images of women by choosing to translate idealized versions or by rewriting what they find in their sources. The ideal is above the real and hence also beyond culture's reach and censure.

4

WOMEN OF THE JACOBEAN COURT DEFENDING THEIR SEX

The Jacobean period was a time of advances in the status of women. Comparing it to earlier periods, Retha Warnicke states that it is the one most deserving the label 'golden.'[1] Many more women than before were receiving some form of education, and more female precedents had been established in publishing and patronizing books. The theatre was paying more attention to women, and though most dramatists simply exploited the gender issue, some were questioning traditional notions.[2] The court itself was relaxing its restrictions, despite the fact that King James himself was a misogynist. Neither his attitude nor the association of the theatre with loose morals kept James's Queen Consort, Anne of Denmark, from appearing in extravagant court masques and inviting other women of the nobility to do the same. Indeed, the Jacobean court appears to have served as a kind of training ground for at least two outspoken women writers – Aemilia Lanyer and Lady Mary Wroth. Lanyer was the daughter and wife of court musicians, while Wroth was the wife of a courtier and lady-in-waiting to Queen Anne of Denmark. The court was undoubtedly a formative environment for these two women. The confidence in public debate and the manoeuvring skills they display may be largely attributed to it. The court was also a source of powerful friends and acquaintances who were called upon by Lady Wroth to give moral support when scandal broke out and by Aemilia Lanyer to provide literary patronage. In their private lives the two women appear to have been nonconformists: loquacious and active, mothers of illegitimate children. In their published works they are obviously critical of patriarchal attitudes and ideas but, as in the case of other women writers, what they finally say is limited by their aims in writing and by established ideologies.

AEMILIA LANYER: CRITICIZING MEN VIA RELIGION

Lanyer was apparently an assertive and unconventional woman. According to Forman, the astrologer whom she visited frequently, she was 'very brave in youth,' 'high-minded,' unable to keep secrets, and had 'many false conceptions.'[3] Her father died bankrupt when she was very young. Later she became the mistress of Lord Chamberlain but, left pregnant by him, was 'for colour' married to Alfonso Lanyer, a court musician who 'spent and consumed her goods.'[4] At court she seems to have been a favourite with many prominent men and women, including Queen Elizabeth.

In 1611 Lanyer published a small book entitled, *Salve Deus Rex Judaeorum*, which Betty Travitsky aptly describes as 'societal rather than religious in purpose.'[5] In addition to the title poem on Christ's passion and death, the book contains nine dedications, two addresses to the reader, and 'A Description of Cook-ham,' a country-house poem celebrating Lady Cumberland's residence. The economic difficulties Lanyer experienced as well as the blatant appeals in her work indicate that, like Whitney, she turned to writing for economic reasons. But unlike Whitney who counted on the popularity of the material she published, Lanyer placed her bid on patronage and specifically on female patronage: all nine of her dedicatees are women of high social rank. Dedication by and to women had become a culturally accepted practice with several precedents. Young Elizabeth Tudor, for example, had translated, dedicated, and presented as gift to her stepmother, Catherine Parr, Marguerite de Navarre's *Miroir*. Anne Locke had also dedicated her translation of a religious work to a woman, Catherine Brandon. The use, too, of multiple dedications was not uncommon. Spenser had appended seventeen dedicatory sonnets to his *Faerie Queene*.

Such precedents could legitimate Lanyer's use of dedication, but they could not likewise endorse her attempt to pose as a professional writer. Though offered *by* women, patronage was not open *to* them. Denied the right to authorship, a woman could

SALVE DEVS

REX IVDÆORVM.

Containing,

1 The Paſsion of Chriſt.

2 Eues Apologie in defence of Women.

3 The Teares of the Daughters of Ieruſalem.

4 The Salutation and Sorrow of the Virgine
Marie.

With diuers other things not vnfit to be read.

Written by Miſtris *Æmilia Lanyer*, Wife to Captaine
Alfonſo Lanyer Seruant to the
Kings Maieſtie.

AT LONDON

Printed by *Valentine Simmes* for *Richard Bonian*, and are
to be ſold at his Shop in Paules Churchyard, at the
Signe of the Floure de Luce and
Crowne. 1 6 1 1.

Figure 4.1 Title page of Aemilia Lanyer's *Salve Deus Rex Judaeorum*
(London, 1611).

not easily ask people to reward financially an activity that was considered rebellious in the first place. For Lanyer, then, as for other women who wrote for publication, gaining acceptance as a female writer was a precondition for, as well as a means to, achieving various aims. In the religious stories she judiciously chooses to rewrite and in her numerous dedications, opposition to cultural norms appears to be inevitably circumscribed by the use of the oppositional voice as a strategy in soliciting patronage.

Respectability, religion, and patronage

The strategies Lanyer uses to establish her acceptance as writer are a combination of male and female literary practices. One of these strategies, used by Whitney also, involves the deployment of conventional notions of respectability. Sometimes in unsubtle ways, Lanyer utilizes available opportunities to prove that she is a person worthy of respect and attention. She starts in fact from the title page itself where she displays her marital and social credentials: 'Written by Mistris Aemilia Lanyer, Wife to Captaine Alfonso Lanyer, Servant to the. Kings Majestie.' Likewise, she turns her acquaintance with some of her dedicatees into opportunities for showing that she has held the attention of the virtuous and the great. There are two obvious examples. One is her strategic mention in the dedication to Queen Anne of the special favours she received from the late Queen Elizabeth. Another is her reference to her association with famous religious households, noticeable particularly in the dedication 'To the Ladie Susan, Countesse Dowager of Kent, and daughter to the Duchesse of Suffolke.' In this piece, Lanyer calls attention to the fact that her dedicatee is 'The noble guide of my ungovern'd dayes' and also the daughter of the well-known Protestant martyr. Thus, without actually lying about her association with any of the women she hopes to impress and profit from, Lanyer draws on the advantages that their respectable names offer to her.

Lanyer's praise of conventional virtues in her dedicatees also helps to credit herself and thus to establish her respectable status. Goodness, piety, love of God, patience, bounty, grace, and moral purity ('a mind . . . free from giving cause/Of least suspect')[6] are among the attributes held up for admiration. Also, the general quality of *virtue* (especially in the sense of worth, excellence, or moral goodness) is frequently mentioned, as it was in most Renaissance dedications. By using such conventional laudatory language, Lanyer appears to endorse the values that this language praises. Hence, she can also claim the benefits of respectability that derive from it. This is not to say that Lanyer is indiscriminate in the type of feminine attributes she is willing to appear to uphold. Indeed, the absences in the text reveal as much as the presences, and the quality of *obedience*, so highly valued by contemporary theoreticians on feminine conduct, is markedly absent. The word itself occurs only once, as an attribute of Christ. Its near opposite, the word 'unsubjected,' rarely found in women's writings and emphatically unfeminine in conventional language at the time, is used as a term of praise for the Duchess of Suffolk who actively opposed religious oppression (p. 53). Indeed, as a relatively independent woman, the only subjection Lanyer seems to have accepted is that to God, to whom she refers as 'the husband of thy [Lady Margaret's] soule.' Likewise, the displacement of the husband as an authority figure is suggested by Lady Margaret's relationship to Christ, who 'dying made her Dowager of all' (B1r). Such references would be appropriate for the dowager Countess, but they could, inadvertently, also undermine the God–husband–wife relationship established by humanists and reformers.

The portrait of Lady Cumberland, the principal dedicatee of the book, offers the best example of how Lanyer employs culturally esteemed feminine virtues and respectable names to establish credibility and gain acceptance among her audience. It is also an example of how the language of patronage, already conventionalized by male writers, shaped Lanyer's work. As the author herself announces in the opening to her poem on the Passion, one of her principal tasks is 'to write [the Countess's] never dying fame' (A1r). Lanyer does this by constructing a mythologized portrait of her subject. The Countess is presented as a pious, almost saintly person. She is compared to a number of great women (including Cleopatra, Sheba, Deborah, Judith, and Joachim's wife) and is shown to be superior to them in faithfulness, devotion, chastity, moral purity, and spiritual strength. Lady Cumberland is presented above all as a woman solely devoted to Christ and unconcerned about the worldly aspects of life:

The meditation of this Monarchs love,
Drawes thee from caring what this world can yield;
Of joyes and griefes both equall thou dost prove,
They have no force, to force thee from the field:
....
Thou from the Court to the Countrie art retir'd,
Leaving the world, before the world leaves thee:
That great Enchantresse of weake mindes admir'd.

(A3v)

No worldly thing can thy faire mind remove;
    Thy faith, thy prayers, and his speciall grace
    Doth open Heav'n, where thou behold'st his face.

(F2r)

Respecting worldly wealth to be but drosse,
Which, if abuz'd, doth proove the owners losse.

(F3r)

Him hast thou truely served all thy life,
And for his love, liv'd with the world at strife.

(G3v)

This representation of the Countess draws both on the language of religious devotion and on that of patronage. But it bears very little relation to the actual person Lanyer attempts to praise. What we know about Lady Cumberland[7] indicates that though she was a woman with religious principles, she was by no means removed from worldly concerns or activities and certainly not disdainful of worldly possessions and titles, as she is made to appear in Salve Deus. Her devotion was not solely to Christ but also to a life-long litigation over the restitution of her husband's property to her daughter Anne.[8] In fact, her biographers inform us that she pursued this matter, which apparently occupied most of the latter part of her life, with unrelenting determination. Also, her application to the Crown for a patent to obtain sea coal and to use it in smelting iron[9] suggests an enterprising spirit as well as a concern for enlarging her possessions. It is true that she left the city and the court to go to the country, but Lanyer's praise of the Countess's country retirement has probably more to do with an emerging literature on the subject of country life than with the Countess's wishes to be removed from the world of strife.[10] In her younger years, Lady Margaret had in fact resented having to move to her husband's residence in the north, while in her later life she was too well established there and had too many possessions at stake to relocate permanently to the city. And we know that she visited the court frequently even after her move from the capital.

This discrepancy between fact and literary representation was not peculiar to Lanyer. Indeed, the importance of Lanyer's portraits lies precisely in the fact that they are not original. Their language is the sycophantic idiom of male writers who wrote for patronage, and especially for female patrons. If we compare, for example, Breton's picture of Mary Herbert as a spiritual being in *The Countesse of Pembrokes Love*[11] we will see that it has much in common with Lanyer's representation of the Countess of Cumberland in *Salve Deus*. In writing for patronage, therefore, Lanyer is using institutionalized language shaped by and for men.

Lanyer's principal strategy in rendering her work profitably acceptable involves the appropriation of religion. This is not, however, a statement about Lanyer's personal religious convictions. Although one could easily argue that Lanyer's outlook, as seen in her work, is not deeply religious,[12] my main point here is that belief in religion did not preclude its appropriation for other purposes. On the contrary, it made it more likely and more convincing. For women authors, religion was a general licence that they used, consciously or unconsciously, to do a number of things which could not easily be done otherwise. For Lanyer specifically, inscription within the religious area meant permission to request certain things from the audience as well as a way out of the binds of culture and class.

First, the religious subject of the passion of Christ, which actually occupies only about one-third of the title poem and a much smaller part of the whole volume, allows Lanyer to circumvent the barrier of social class. Addressing an aristocratic audience involved a liberty that an untitled woman could not as a matter of course take in the sixteenth or early seventeenth century, and Lanyer seems to have been particularly class conscious. As her astrologer tells us, in actual life she was very anxious to acquire a title: she demanded to know 'whether she should be a Lady or no.'[13] This anxiety, manifested in various forms, is evident throughout her book. In her epistle 'To all vertuous Ladies in generall' she apologizes for placing ordinary women 'In generall tearmes . . . with the rest,/ Whom Fame commends to be the very best' (b4r). And in her 'Description of Cooke-ham,' she regrets the social distance that separates her from her aristocratic female friends, Lady Margaret and Lady Anne:

> Unconstant Fortune, thou art most too blame,
> Who casts us downe into so lowe a frame:
> Where our great friends we cannot dayly see,
> So great difference is there in degree.
>
> (H3v̇)

It is within this context that we must read Lanyer's repeated references to Christ's humble birth:

> Loe here thy great Humility was found,
> Beeing King of Heaven, and Monarch of the Earth
> Yet well content to have thy Glory drownd,
> By beeing counted of so meane a berth.
>
> (B4v)

> Unto the Meane he makes the Mightie bow,
> And raiseth up the Poore out of the dust.
>
> (A3r)

Within the same context, we must also read Lanyer's praise of Lady Cumberland as a lover of the low-born Jesus:

> Then how much more art thou to be commended,
> That seek'st thy love in lowly shepheards weed?
> A seeming Trades-mans sonne, of none attended,
> Save of a few in povertie and need.
>
> (G3v)

Apparently, then, the religious subject of the poem, with its focus on the passion of low-born Christ, allows Lanyer to enter the company of women of aristocratic birth and hence to establish a socially legitimate speaking voice. (The idea of God or Christ as a leveller, who 'makes the Mightie bow, And raiseth up the Poore out of the dust,' was also used by women petitioners and preachers of the revolutionary period.)

The religious subject proved even more useful in soliciting patronage. Indeed, the deployment of the story of Christ as a marketable subject is quite apparent. In many cases, it is blatantly treated as a selling point:

[To Lady Arabella]
                              spare one looke
Upon this humbled King, who all forsooke,
    That in his dying armes he might imbrace
    Your beauteous Soule, and fill it with his grace.

                                                        (p. 52)

[To the Countess of Bedford]
Loe here he coms all stucke with pale deaths arrows:
    In whose most precious wounds your soule may reade
    Salvation, while he (dying Lord) doth bleed.
You whose cleare Judgement farre exceeds my skil,
Vouchsafe to entertain this dying lover.

                                                        (C1r)

[To the Countess of Cumberland]
Sometimes h'appeares to thee in Shepheards weed,
And so presents himselfe before thine eyes,
A good old man; that goes his flocke to feed;
Thy colour changes, and thy heart doth rise;
Thou call'st, he comes, thou find'st tis he indeed,
Thy Soule conceaves that he is truely wise:
    Nay more, desires that he may be the Booke,
    Whereon thine eyes continually may looke.
Sometime imprison'd, naked, poore, and bare,
Full of diseases, impotent, and lame,
Blind, deafe, and dumbe, he comes unto his faire,
To see if yet shee will remaine the same;
Nay sicke and wounded, now thou do'st prepare
To cherish him in thy deare Lovers name:
    Yea thou bestow'st all paines, all cost, all care,
    That may relieve him, and his health repaire.

                                                        (F2r)

The last two stanzas quoted above suggest that the religious subject of the poem also allowed Lanyer to utilize the Christian concept of good deeds[14] in soliciting economic support for herself. At various points in the title poem, as in the passage cited below, Lanyer praises Lady Cumberland for her religious devotion and for the material proof of it:

Shee sacrificeth to her deerest Love [Christ],
With flowers of Faith, and garlands of Good deeds,

....

Shee attendeth upon him, and his flocke shee feeds.

(F3v)

In the dedicatory epistle to Lady Anne, Lanyer argues, rather self-righteously, that economic support for the unprivileged should be required as proof of noble birth, challenging in the process the concept of hereditary aristocracy. But even in that instance, she falls back on the connection between social class and religion: 'Gods Stewards must for all the poore provide,/If in Gods house they purpose to abide' (C2v).

Religion and the defence of women

Lanyer's unmistakable female voice constitutes the unconventional part of her work. It serves both as a form of protest against misogynist ideas and as an additional strategy for attracting patronesses.

Her strongest and most detailed statements on women and patriarchy are found in two parts of *Salve Deus*: in the epistle 'To the Vertuous Reader' and in 'Eves Apologie in defence of Women.' These two pieces and partly also the dedicatory epistle to Queen Anne place Lanyer among the few female critics of her culture. The most striking one in boldness and directness is the epistle to the reader. I cite a large portion of it here:

I have written this small volume. . . . And this have I done, to make knowne to the world, that all women deserve not to be blamed though some forgetting they are women themselves, and in danger to be condemned by the wordes of their owne mouthes, fall into so great an errour, as to speak unadvisedly against the rest of their sexe; which if it be true, I am perswaded they can shew their own imperfection in nothing more: and therefore could wish . . . to be practised by evill disposed men, who forgetting they were borne of women, nourished of women, and . . . doe like Vipers deface the wombes wherein they were

TO THE VERTVOVS
Reader.

Ften haue I heard, that it is the property of some women, not only to emulate the virtues and perfections
of the rest, but also by all their powers of ill speaking,
to ecclipse the brightnes of their deserued fame: now
contrary to this custome, which men I hope vniustly lay to
their charge, I haue written this small volume, or little booke,
for the generall vse of all virtuous Ladies and Gentlewomen
of this kingdome; and in commendation of some particular
persons of our owne sexe, such as for the most part, are so well
knowne to my selfe, and others, that I dare vndertake Fame
dares not to call any better. And this haue I done, to make
knowne to the world, that all women deserue not to be blamed
though some forgetting they are women themselues, and in
danger to be condemned by the words of their owne mouthes,
fall into so great an errour, as to speake vnaduisedly against
the rest of their sexe; which if it be true, I am perswaded they
can shew their owne imperfection in nothing more: and therefore could wish (for their owne ease, modesties, and credit) they
would referre such points of folly, to be practised by euill disposed men, who forgetting they were borne of women, nourished
of women, and that if it were not by the means of women, they
would be quite extinguished out of the world, and a finall ende
of them all, doe like Vipers deface the wombes, wherein they
were bred, onely to giue way and vtterance to their want of
discretion and goodnesse. Such as these, were they that disho-
noured Christ his Apostles and Prophets, putting them to
shamefull deaths. Therefore we are not to regard any imputations, that they vndeseruedly lay vpon vs, no otherwise than
to make vse of them to our owne benefits, as spurres to vertue, making vs flie all occasions that may colour their vniust.

f 3   speeches

Figure 4.2 Facsimile of the two-page epistle entitled 'To the Vertuous
Reader' contained in the first printing of *Salve Deus*.

speeches to passe currant. Especially considering that they haue tempted euen the patience of God himselfe, who gaue power to wise and virtuous women, to bring downe their pride and arrogancie. As was cruell Cesarus *by the discreet counsell of noble* Deborah, *Iudge and Prophetesse of Israel : and resolution of* Iael *wife of Heber the Kenite : wicked* Haman, *by the diuine prayers and prudent proceedings of beautifull* Hester : *blasphemous* Holofernes, *by the inuincible courage, rare wisdome, and confident carriage of* Iudeth : *& the vniust Indges, by the innocency of chast* Susanna : *with infinite others, which for breuitie sake I will omit. As also in respect it pleased our Lord and Sauiour Iesus Christ, without the assistance of man, beeing free from originall and all other sinnes, from the time of his conception, till the houre of his death, to be begotten of a woman : borne of a woman, nourished of a woman, obedient to a woman; and that he healed woman, pardoned women, comforted women : yea, euen when he was in his greatest agonie and bloodie sweat, going to be crucified, and also in the last houre of his death, tooke care to dispose of a woman : after his resurrection, appeared first to a woman, sent a woman to declare his most glorious resurrection to the rest of his Disciples. Many other examples I could alleadge of diuers faithfull and virtuous women, who haue in all ages, not onely beene Confessors, but also indured most cruel martyrdome for their faith in Iesus Christ. All which is sufficient to inforce all good Christians and honourable minded men to speake reuerently of our sexe, and especially of all virtuous and good women. To the modest sensures of both which, I refer these my imperfect indeauours, knowing that according to their owne excellent dispositions, they will rather, cherish, nourish, and increase the least sparke of virtue where they find it, by their fauourable and best interpretations, than quench it by wrong constructions. To whom I wish all increase of virtue, and desire their best opinions.*

bred. . . . Therefore we are not to regard any imputations,
that they undeservedly lay upon us, no otherwise than to
make use of them to our owne benefits, as spurres to vertue,
making us flie all occasions that may colour their unjust
speeches to passe currant. Especially considering that they
have tempted even the patience of God himself, who gave
power to wise and virtuous women, to bring down their
pride and arrogancie.

(pp. 77–8)

The importance of this piece of criticism lies primarily in two
facts: its presence in a book addressed to noblewomen and
its foregrounding of the lack of solidarity among women. In
pointing to this latter issue, Lanyer is locating one of the major
setbacks in the status of women in the early modern period.
As a whole, however, this piece, like Jane Anger's *Protection*
and other defences of women, is basically conformist. Women's
problem is presented mainly as bad faith on the part of men, and
the solution proposed is for women to refrain from provoking
men's criticism. Implicitly, women are asked to comply with the
rules that reproduce their subordination. Thus, not only from
our point of view today but also from that of later seventeenth-
century feminist tracts, like *Womens Sharpe Revenge*, Lanyer's
statements here are basically conservative, failing to consider
matters of economics and culture. (See Simon Shepherd's
modern edition of four pamphlets, *The Women's Sharp Revenge*,
including Anger's *Protection*.)

But while in the epistle to the reader Lanyer states the problem
simplistically and does not articulate any of the fundamental
problems in the construction of gender, in 'Eves Apologie in
defence of Women' she does. In this piece, which is incorporated
into the story of the Passion of Christ, she treats several subtle
but crucial issues and shows that if she cannot see into all
the workings of her culture, she is at least sharply aware of
the way patriarchy has oppressed women. Lanyer first locates
one of the main strategies used by western patriarchal culture
in the subjugation of the female sex: she shows how certain
biblical incidents have been selected, at the exclusion of others,
and used to represent woman as the cause of man's fall and
destruction. She then employs the same strategy, but with a
different selection of incidents, to show that the loss of Eden

was actually Adam's responsibility, and that men trangressed more gravely by crucifying Christ.

In arguing for Eve's innocence, Lanyer points out that since Adam was charged with authority, he should be the one held responsible for his own as well as for the actions of his subordinate wife:

> But surely Adam cannot be excus'd,
> Her fault though great, yet he was most too blame;
> What Weaknesse offerd, Strength might have refus'd,
> Being Lord of all, the greater was his shame:
> Although the Serpents craft had her abus'd,
> Gods holy word ought all his actions frame,
>   For he was Lord and King of all the earth,
>   Before poore Eve had either life or breath.
>
> Who being fram'd by Gods eternall hand,
> The perfect'st man that ever breath'd on earth,
> And from Gods mouth receiv'd that strait command,
> The breach whereof he knew was present death:
> Yea having powre to rule both Sea and Land,
> Yet with one Apple wonne to loose that breath,
>   Which God hath breathed in his beauteous face,
>   Bringing us all in danger and disgrace.
>
> (D1r)

Here and in the rest of her argument, Lanyer points to the bias involved in the male reading of the Bible: responsibility is portioned out equally but authority is not; men want it both ways – Adam's authority over Eve and Eve's autonomy in the fall. She implies that if the balance of power is to be unequal, if the authority for actions taken is to be given to the man, then the responsibility for these actions must follow the same chain of command and must therefore go to the one invested with authority. Thus in what appears to be a naïve way, Lanyer discloses and exploits the biases and contradictions she sees in long-standing patriarchal arguments.

Lanyer's case in support of Eve's innocence is skilfully linked to her argument about man's sin in crucifying Christ. She cleverly establishes a parallel between Adam and Eve on the one hand and Pontius Pilate and his wife on the other, in order to prove the similarity of the situations and man's position on the erring side in the latter pair. She discloses Pilate's political motives in giving up Christ (including his fear of 'Peoples threatnings . . ./That he to Caesar could not be a friend, /Unlesse he sent sweet JESUS to his end,' (D3r)) and at the same time points to the wisdom of Pilate's wife, who advised her husband to 'have nothing to doe at all/With that just man,' (D2r). Furthermore, she suggests, even if Eve did err, men's sin in the crucifixion makes woman's original error seem lighter:

> Till now your indiscretion sets us free,
> And makes our former fault much lesse appeare.
>
> (D1r)

In the conclusion to her argument, Lanyer addresses men directly, challenges what she sees as self-assumed, unwarranted, and tyrannical authority on their part, and asks for women's freedom:

> Then let us have our Libertie againe,
> And challendge to your selves no Sov'raigntie;
> You came not in the world without our paine,
> Make that a barre against your crueltie;
> Your fault beeing greater, why should you disdaine
> Our beeing your equals, free from tyranny?
> If one weake woman simply did offend,
> This sinne of yours, hath no excuse, nor end.
>
> (D2r)

Lanyer's argument about men's sin in the crucifixion is given force by the female characteristics of the Christ she portrays. A victim in the hands of tyrannical authority, Christ is a man with passive qualities usually expected of women:

> If zeale, if grace, if love, if pietie,
> If constancie, if faith, if faire obedience,
> If valour, patience, or sobrietie;
> If chast behaviour, meekenesse, continence,
> If justice, mercie, bountie, charitie,
> Who can compare with his Divinitie?
>
> (p. 71)

Christ's appearance is likewise marked by feminine characteristics:

116

This is that Bridegroome that appeares so faire,
So sweet, so lovely in his Spouses sight,
That unto Snowe we may his face compare,
His cheekes like skarlet, and his eyes so bright
As purest Doves that in the rivers are,
Washed with milke, to give the more delight;
　His head is likened to the finest gold,
　His curled lockes so beauteous to behold;
Black as a Raven in her blackest hew;
His lips like skarlet threeds, yet much more sweet
Than is the sweetest hony dropping dew,
Or hony combes, where all the Bees doe meet;
Yea, he is constant, and his words are true,
His cheeckes are beds of spices, flowers sweet;
　His lips like Lillies, dropping downe pure mirrhe,
　Whose love, before all worlds we doe preferre.

(F1v)

The association of Christ with femaleness apparently derives from medieval times. In iconographic and textual sources, Christ's body and experiences were sometimes identified with female functions.[15] His saving role was seen as analogous to giving birth and feeding, and his bleeding wound was associated with lactating. Medieval female mystics in particular describe Christ's body in terms that suggest a subjective experience and an identification with the suffering male divinity. Julian of Norwich 'identifies Christ's pains on the cross with a woman's pains in childbirth, and his love with the "intimate, willing and dependable" services our mothers do for us.'[16] Catherine of Siena speaks of attaching 'ourselves to the breast of Christ crucified, which is the source of charity, and by means of that flesh we draw milk.'[17] These and other religious women of the Middle Ages describe Christ's life in emotional and dramatic images which link it to the female experience. Lanyer apparently draws on such images. What becomes interesting therefore is not the originality of the posture of a feminized Christ but the fact that Lanyer deploys such a posture. Like medieval women, Lanyer appropriates a powerful religious symbol, turning it into an uncontroversial vehicle for expressing her own anger and opposition to tyrannical authority. The story of the Passion allows her to speak about as well as for the oppressed subject.

In her poem, Jesus's confrontation with authority is described as a confrontation between powerless subject and oppressor:

> Yet could their learned Ignorance apprehend
> No light of grace, to free themselves from blame:
> Zeale, Lawes, Religion, now they doe pretend
> Against the truth, untruths they seeke to frame:
> Now al their powres, their wits, their strengths, they
> > Against one siely, weake, unarmed man, bend
> > Who no resistance makes, though much he can.
>
> > > (C1v)

These and similar passages stress the violence committed on a passive subject and also reveal Lanyer's awareness of how powerful social institutions (law, religion, education) could be wielded to oppress subjects deviating from the established norm. She apparently saw not only the religious but also the political side of the biblical events of the story. (I have already mentioned her political analysis of Pilate's actions.)

Patronage and feminism

Like Jane Anger, Rachel Speght, and a number of other female authors, Lanyer defends women against male charges and establishes a spirit of solidarity even by addressing herself to women only. On this account, that is, in a historically specific sense, Lanyer could be called a feminist. This is not to say that she is consistent in her feminist voice – for she is not, and could not have been. Sometimes she thrusts out challenging feminist statements while usually she retreats into conventional language; still other times she seems to occupy a middle ground, expressing self-righteousness through a feminized Christ. Why is there such a divergence or inconsistency? What is the purpose of what would have been considered then an outright attack on men in a book so obviously aimed to solicit support from women patrons?

The problem of inconsistency is to a large extent a function of language and history. If Lanyer is in places inconsistent, so are the discourses she employs. Even so, I suggest that in her case the inconsistency is partly due to the author's own unease, uncertainty, and confusion about her expressions of female solidarity. Despite her occasional bold declarations, the text discloses that Lanyer does not know how exactly to treat the women she addresses, or what benefits she may expect from adopting what might be called a feminist speaking voice within a female group. In other words, she does not appear certain that feminism is an efficacious strategy in soliciting female patronage. In the title poem of *Salve Deus* the defence of women drifts into praise of the Countess of Cumberland in conventional terms. The Countess is presented as an embodiment of sixteenth-century admired virtues. Indeed, one might argue that in the latter part of the poem the feminist spirit becomes somewhat offset by the Countess's portrait, for in praising Lady Cumberland, Lanyer seems not only to espouse conventional virtues but also to deprecate a number of other women. Cleopatra, Deborah, Judith, and Sheba, among other female figures, are presented as inferior to the Countess. The author uses them not just to enlarge the circle of 'good women'[18] but to flatter the Countess. It seems that as she approaches the end of her volume (and as the book becomes more exclusively directed to Lady Cumberland and Lady Anne), Lanyer drops her feminist voice. If the praise of the male saints at the end of the poem is an attempt at offering a counterweight to the earlier unflattering picture of men,[19] then in the context of what I have been saying, it seems very doubtful that such an attempt can be read as a token of the author's concern about being unfair to men. The praise of these male saints has probably more to do with Lanyer's doubts about her feminist strategy than with her conscience. In this case (especially if those particular saints were the Countess's favourites), it might be an abandonment of feminism in favour of a more profitable approach. In 'A Description of Cook-ham,' which is Lanyer's most promising bid for patronage, she refrains from what might then be considered bold statements in favour of women. This, taken together with the absence of such statements from the dedicatory epistles to Lady Margaret and Lady Anne, suggests perhaps that the feminist sentiments of the principal potential patronesses of the book could not be taken as granted or used in public. Although these two women had grudges against men that Lanyer could appreciate and exploit, she could not with certainty enlarge them into a public castigation of the male sex.

In this context, the fluctuations in the feminist voice of the text reflect the author's discursive impasse as well as her attempt to contain what might offend if carried too far. In some cases, apparently it did offend. The British Library copy shows that the aggressive epistle 'To the Vertuous Reader' was removed along with four dedications when the book was reissued in the same year it was published. Although we do not know the reasons for the removal of each of these dedications,[20] it seems almost certain that the epistle to the reader was removed because of its feminist content. Apparently, the women to whom the book was addressed objected to its bold statements. And could some have objected even to the milder feminist portions (like 'Eves Apologie') or to their names being used by a woman who turned out to be more than just a writer of religious stories? The omission of the dedications to the Countesses of Pembroke, Kent, and Suffolk points to this possibility, especially if these dedications were *ex post facto*. It cannot be merely a coincidence that the dedicatory epistles which remained in the volume are to women who either had promised to support Lanyer (as is probably the case with Lady Cumberland and Lady Anne) or did not care about the association of their name with feminist ideas. Most likely, Queen Anne belonged to this latter category. More flamboyant in her behaviour than most English noblewomen, Anne of Denmark generally disregarded criticisms aimed at her feminine improprieties. In Lanyer's book the dedication to her is the only one that contains at least some overtly feminist lines (see A4r). Thus from the available evidence it seems that Lanyer miscalculated the extent to which she could employ feminist sentiment to her advantage. In her culture, feminism and respectability were not compatible. Nor could a woman who fostered feminist notions assume that other women around her shared these notions.

As a woman writer trying to squeeze into an already over-crowded and somewhat outworn system of patronage for men, Lanyer has very little room for manoeuvre. Her religious subject gives her an opportunity to get a foot in the door, but her appeal to sisterhood seems to have been a miscalculated tactic. Addressing a group of eminent and respectable noblewomen was not easy. The lack of solidarity that the epistle 'To the Vertuous Reader' brings to the fore had much deeper roots and greater magnitude than Lanyer – herself enmeshed in the ideas and material practices of her culture – could probably see.

MARY WROTH: BLAMING TYRANNICAL
FATHERS AND INCONSTANT LOVERS

In an earlier chapter it was stated that Renaissance women of the upper classes suffered greater restrictions; that transgression on the part of noblewomen could jeopardize both their reputation and livelihood. This seems to have obtained in the 1620s also, but some aristocratic families were apparently loosening up in their attitudes towards women. Lady Mary Wroth, though in some respects atypical of her female contemporaries, exemplifies both the opportunities and the limitations which women writers in general and those of noble birth in particular were encountering in the early seventeenth century.

Wroth was one of the most prolific women writers of the Renaissance. She wrote a long work of prose fiction (*Urania*, 1621), a considerable amount of secular love poetry which includes a complete sonnet sequence from a woman's point of view (*Pamphilia to Amphilanthus*, 1621), and a pastoral play (*Love's Victorie*, unpublished).[21] According to her editor, Josephine Roberts, Lady Mary possessed an 'independent spirit'[22] and, as her public defence of the *Urania* shows, she also possessed confidence and assertiveness. She had a liberal education, with much encouragement from her family, especially from her father, Robert Sidney, who was quite proud of Mary's aptitude in learning, though he did not take her training as seriously as he took that of his sons.[23] When she was young she accompanied her mother on several trips to the continent, and later, back home, she participated in court entertainments.[24] Along with Queen Anne of Denmark and other noblewomen she acted in several court masques, including *The Masque of Blackness* by Ben Jonson and Inigo Jones.

She was closely acquainted with leading literary men, like Jonson and John Davies of Hereford, who paid much attention to her, not least because she was the niece of the famous Sir Philip Sidney and the Countess of Pembroke. Jonson very clearly associates her with her literary heritage in one of his epigrams,[25] and another contemporary, Joshua Silvester, refers to her as a Sidney 'In whom her Uncles noble Veine renews.'[26] Lady Mary did not discourage such associations with her literary relatives. On the contrary, she identified with her parental ancestors, as the use of the Sidney coat of arms reveals, and drew on the benefits of such an identification.

Unlike her talented but timid aunt, the Countess of Pembroke, Lady Mary turned her family's great name into a licence to write and publish. The name of Sidney could serve as both an advertisement and a shield of protection. The full title of her romance provides a clear indication: *The Countesse of Montgomeries Urania. Written by the right honourable the Lady Mary Wroath. Daughter to the right Noble Robert Earle of Leicester And Neece to the ever famous, and renowned Sr Phillips Sidney knight. And to the most excelent Lady Mary Countesse of Pembroke late deceased.*[27] Besides displaying the family credentials, the title is also meant to echo that of Sidney's romance, *The Countess of Pembroke's Arcadia*, which had already gained great popularity and which Wroth uses as a literary model. Thus venturing into public view was not as difficult for the niece of Sir Philip and Mary Sidney as it might have been for women of lesser literary heritage.

However, there were limitations and restrictions. One of them was the literary legacy itself. Lady Mary apparently felt safer to write in genres that, though long out of vogue, had been favoured and explored by various members of the Sidney family, and principally by her uncle Sir Philip. In her pastoral romance she follows Sidney's style of interspersing songs and poems in the prose, and in her sonnet sequence *Pamphilia to Amphilanthus* she borrows strategies and phrases from *Astrophil and Stella*, and possibly also from her father's sonnets. She does not of course slavishly imitate the forms she inherits. She contributes to the sonnet genre by employing a female persona and reversing the conventional roles of lover and beloved, and by shifting the focus away from the latter. Unlike conventional sonneteers, Wroth does not idealize the beloved or seek to praise his physical charms; she is more interested in the psychological state of the female lover and the concept of constancy. And as Roberts notes, her tone resembles Donne's in its cynicism.[28] None the less, it is important to note that Wroth's family tradition both encouraged her to write and prevented her from venturing into new literary ground.

Still, this limitation was relatively small in comparison with other, more tangible ones. Certain events in Mary Wroth's life show the kind of factors that negatively influenced and eventually suppressed her work.

At eighteen, Lady Mary agreed to marry Sir Robert Wroth, the son of a wealthy landowner. The marriage, which her parents had arranged and for which they had paid £1,000, did not turn out to be a successful one.[29] Yet in this particular case even an unhappy marital situation would have been less damaging than widowhood, for when Sir Robert died in 1614 he left her with a debt of £23,000, a one-month-old son, and a jointure of £1,200. This financial predicament (not unlike the one Aemilia Lanyer was left in by her husband) worsened two years later with her son's death, which caused the jointure to revert to Sir Robert's brother, John Wroth. The two illegitimate children that Lady Mary bore to her cousin, William Herbert, Third Earl of Pembroke, did not help matters either financially or socially. Josephine Roberts remarks that 'even in the licentious atmosphere of the Jacobean court,' the birth of illegitimate children would create a scandal and she attributes Lady Mary's decline in her role as a leading female courtier to this fact.[30] Yet the most damaging blow to Mary Wroth came with the publication of the *Urania* and the storm of accusations she received on account of it.

The Denny incident and the suppression of Wroth's book

When the *Urania* appeared in 1621, its author was severely criticized for its thinly disguised satiric treatment of court intrigues and family affairs of the nobility.[31] John Chamberlain wrote to Dudley Carlton that Wroth 'takes great libertie or rather license to traduce whom she please, and thinks she dances in a net.' Another man, Sir Aston Cokayne, remarked in one of his poems that 'The Lady Wrothe's Urania is repleat/With elegancies, but too full of heat.' The greatest havoc yet was caused by one powerful noble, Edward Denny, Baron Waltham and later Earl of Norwich, who found a satiric portrait of his family in the book's incident of Serilius. A bitter battle ensued between Wroth who denied the allegations and Denny who insisted in his charges. Accusatory poems and letters were exchanged,[32] Denny calling her a 'hermaphrodite' and telling her to leave 'idle books alone/For wise and worthyer women have writte none,' and Wroth attacking his uncontrollable

The
Countesse
of Mountgomeries
URANIA.
Written by the right honorable the Lady
MARY WROATH:
Daughter to the right Noble Robert
Earle of Leicester.
And Neece to the ever famous, and re-
nowned S.t Phillips Sidney knight. And to
y.e most excellent Lady Mary Countesse of
Pembroke late deceased.

LONDON
Printed for IOH. MARRIOTT
and IOHN GRISMAND. And
are to bee sould at theire shop-
pes in St Dunstons Churchyard in Fleetstreet and in
Poules Ally at y.e signe of
the Gunn.

1621

Figure 4.3 Title page of Mary Wroth's *The Countess of Montgomery's Urania* (London, 1621).

124

temper and bidding him 'lett railing rimes alone.' The help of powerful friends was sought by both sides. But despite Lady Mary's ability to put up a good fight with a powerful man and her refusal to be intimidated by his terms, she was finally forced to withdraw her book from circulation, shortly after its initial appearance, and to recall the already sold copies. As Carolyn Swift rightly infers, Mary Wroth had more to lose by creating enemies among the administration than to gain from the sale of the book. 'Her own needs and the needs of her two illegitimate children . . . forced her to depend on the king's good will all her life. Every year after 1623 she obtained a royal order protecting her from creditors. Naturally, then, she had to withdraw her book from sale, in spite of her jaunty defence and the hours she spent writing it.'[33]

This incident, along with its consequent suppression of the *Urania*, shows a number of things. It shows first of all how much economics, gender, and class were intertwined; how they could combine with Renaissance ways of reading fiction to suppress a woman's writing.[34] A financially dependent woman who wrote critically of her culture and used source material from her environment had very little chance of survival, in literal or literary terms. And it shows once more how a female writer's choice of genre and treatment of subject matter cannot be properly understood without reference to her sex. As Margaret Witten-Hannah puts it, 'There seems no doubt that some of the scandal can be ascribed to the fact that a woman had dared to write fiction dealing with love and sex, however formally couched in the language of romance.'[35] Denny's choice of language and his reminder, in one of his letters, that Lady Mary's aunt translated 'holy books' and did not write 'lascivious tales and amorous toys,' certainly does link the offence with the author's sex and suggests a more basic transgression.

Yet the Denny affair also clearly shows the combative spirit of Mary Wroth and her determination to fight back on equal terms. Her letters to Denny evidence her refusal to concede even the smallest point. Far from apologizing, she turned his accusations back against him. She denied his allegations vehemently, even though various contemporaries beside him had recognized the satiric nature of her book (the Earl of Rutland even wrote to her asking for an interpretative key), and she had taken little trouble to provide anything more than a thin disguise for the portraits she included.[36] It seems rather that by denying the charges and defending her book, the author was defending her right to criticize what she found objectionable in her culture. An analysis of the *Urania* reveals that she objected especially to her culture's construction of male–female relationships and to men's use of women as objects in social and economic negotiations. Wroth is not sparing in her criticism of men, while she is quite daring in some of her female portraits. The analysis also reveals, however, how very difficult it is even for a woman of Wroth's spirit and education to abandon altogether patriarchal models of femininity and how self-trapping a defensive position can be in a critique of gender ideology.

Charges against fathers and lovers

If there is one thing apparent in the hundreds of adventures and episodes that occupy the 558 folio pages of the published *Urania*, it is that the author sees women's discontent as stemming in large part from patriarchal practices and attitudes. In conventional romances people come for succour to valiant knights who undertake to fight in their cause, but in the *Urania* these people are almost exclusively women who have been victims of love affairs or forced marriages.

Wroth is particularly severe in her attack on fathers, especially among the nobility, and it is not surprising that men like Denny would feel the sting. Sometimes through the use of sarcasm, Wroth castigates fathers for forcing their daughters to marry against their will and affection, disclosing in the process their cruelty, egotism, and crude materialism. The story of Liana (pp. 204–11) illustrates the tyrannical authority that fathers exercise over their daughters. Liana is in love with Alarinus but her father has different plans. He matches her with another man and even demands her consent. The language that the woman uses in telling her story indicates Wroth's points of attack:

> hee would have mee joyne my dutifull agreement to his choice, and order my love to goe along with his pleasure, for young maides eyes should like onely where their Father liked, and love where he did appoint. . . . I besought him

to remember his promise, which was, never to force me against my will, to marry any. Will (said he) why your will ought to be no other then obedience, and in that, you should be rather wilfull in obeying, then question what I appoint; if not, take this, and be assured of it, that if you like not as I like, and wed where I will you, you shall never from me receive least favour, but be accompted a stranger and a lost childe. . . . Who is this fine man hath wonne your idle fancie? Who hath made your duty voide? Whose faire tongue hath brought you to the foulenesse of disobedience? Speake, and speake truely, that I may discerne what choice you can make, to refuse my fatherly authoritie over you.

(p. 207)[37]

Wroth uncovers the supposed paternal care and morality, showing them to be thin disguises for underlying material motives. In the Laurimello incident (pp. 243–5) the father of the woman finds a match for her, but while the arrangements are in progress a better prospect shows up, 'whose estate was greater, and neerer to our dwelling: to which my father (being more than ordinarily affectionate to me) quickly harkned, and willingly embraced' (p. 244). Appealing to his moral values, the woman reminds her father that her honour will be damaged if she is 'thus yeelded to every great match,' but though he recognizes that 'honour [is] as necessary to a womans happy life, as good lungs to a healthful body' (p. 244), he is not willing to back down on the new marriage bargain he has struck.

In these and other similar incidents, paternal authority is associated with tyranny, egotism, and materialism. Consistently excluding mothers from her objects of attack, Wroth identifies oppressive attitudes and practices as patriarchal and shows that fathers, brothers, and husbands are responsible for women's transgression of cultural norms. Without endorsing transgression *per se*, she views sympathetically 'discontented and (so unfortunate) women' who, trapped in unhappy marriages, seek an outlet in extramarital love relationships.[38] Likewise, she is sympathetic to young women who resort to scheming in order to escape undersirable matches. The language Wroth uses to describe such situations often suggests both her close familiarity

127

with the problem in her culture and the extent to which she saw women's scheming, at least in this area, as culturally produced behaviour. Here is an example of a woman describing her attempt to escape her predicament:

> having no meanes, save mine owne industrie, and strength of mind busied like a Spider, which being to crosse from one beame to another, must worke by waies, and goe fare about, making more webs to catch her selfe into her owne purpose, then if she were to goe an ordinary straight course: and so did I, out of my wit weave a web to deceive all, but mine owne desires.
>
> (p. 244)

Such portrayals also register the dialectic between women and dominant culture in the Renaissance – the kind of action and reaction situation that existed between authority and resistance to it. In this kind of conflict, which in the *Urania* always involves matters of love, Wroth encourages disobedience to authority figures. Furthermore, Mary Wroth's treatment, almost exclusively, of the predicament of women in a forced marriage (when in reality sons as well as daughters were subjected to pressure in this matter) indicates both her feminine consciousness and the extent to which she saw such a practice as bearing particularly on women.

Although in places the *Urania* reads like a guide on how to thwart paternal authority, on the whole Wroth appears more concerned with showing the binds for women in a society where men make the rules and make them contradictory at that. The requirements of the father conflict with those of the lover and the woman is trapped in the middle. If she remains faithful to the man she loves and refuses to marry her father's choice, she is accused of disobedience. If she abandons her lover to obey her father, who frequently threatens her with disinheritance, she is charged with inconstancy. Rather than bail her out, Wroth implies, her lover involves her in a worse bind through his inconstancy and hence unreliability. On the one hand he requires her to risk her livelihood in proving her faithfulness to him, while on the other he guarantees nothing in return and more often than not abandons her in the end. Male inconstancy is shown to be one of the principal factors in the binds. In innumerable episodes Wroth portrays the disadvantageous position of the woman who is caught between a tyrannical father or brother on the one hand and a unfaithful lover on the other. The situation is especially disastrous in an extramarital affair. As the following example shows, the woman is the one who suffers all the consequences in the end:

> Then did my husband take a disgracefull course against mee, that Country being very strict in punishment for such offences [i.e., adultery], I was condemn'd, and censur'd, and indur'd my punishment, but then I thought how this man [her lover] for my paines suffered for his sake, I should have found affection or continuance of his love, hee also left mee, and in such case as I have no money or meanes, but to starve for want, my estate being againe seased on by my husband and yeelded him by censure.

> (p. 351)

Wroth is sympathetic towards this woman and others in similar binds,[39] and the fact that they are married does not in her view lessen the responsibility of the male lover to remain constant. In fact, male inconstancy is Wroth's principal criticism of men.

Like Whitney in the *Admonition*, Wroth in the *Urania* reverses the stereotype of women as fickle and changeable. In language that reveals her awareness of the history of the idea she is treating, Wroth voices the problem through one of her female characters, with a touch of irony on the supposed superiority of the male sex:

> It was laid to our charge in times passed to bee false, and changing, but they who excell us in all perfections, would not for their honours sake, let us surpasse them in any one thing, though that, and now are much more perfect, and excellent in that then wee.

> (p. 375)

Through countless episodes as well as through the two principal characters, Pamphilia and Amphilanthus, the author reiterates and proves this point – that women, not men, are the constant sex. In the course of the *Urania*, Pamphilia is shown to remain persistently faithful to an inconstant Amphilanthus ('lover of the two') who abandons her more than once to go off with other love partners. Pamphilia suffers in the process. The point is clear: in a system where women depend on men, emotionally and otherwise, the effects of male inconstancy are negative mainly for the dependants. One of the book's minor characters seems to express the author's sentiment on the matter: 'to whom can harme insue, save to us wretched trusting women' (p. 251).

Wroth shows that men's rules of playing the love game are responsible for at least some of the animosity and intrigue among women. As a female courtier, she herself had no doubt witnessed the vicious schemes of woman against woman in the Jacobean court[40] and had seen them performed on the Jacobean stage. Accordingly, her book contains several examples of jealous and plotting women. Wroth does not appear certain about the causes of this type of behaviour. Sometimes she attributes it to plain malice and ill nature, but other times she suggests that it is caused by men's attitudes. Indeed the *Urania*, unlike conventional romances, abounds in incidents of women fighting for the same man. The story of Dolorindus (pp. 154–9) provides one example. This man, a courtier, falls in love with one woman but he also pays some attention to another. Enraged with jealousy, the women end up accusing each other. His beloved finally withdraws from the whole affair, despite the fact that her husband has meanwhile died, and Dolorindus turns into a misogynist because she will not accept his excuses.

If Wroth shows that women can be hostile to each other on account of men, she also recognizes the bond that exists between them. Unlike earlier chivalric romances (the *Mirrour* and *Amadis de Gaul*, for example) which restricted close female relationships to the heroine-confidante type, the *Urania* shows several instances of supportive friendship between women in various situations.[41] And in the case of Pamphilia and Antissia, Wroth shows that the competition for the love of the same man is not enough to destroy other genuine feelings. The author even envisages, momentarily, the possibility of romantic love between women. A nymph that Pamphilia encounters wonders what it would be like 'first to bee touched by those best deerest lipps, and so to passe into her royall breast' (p. 182), while Pamphilia and Antissia lie together the evening before their parting and in the morning are 'blushingly ashamed so to bee surprized' by the sun and 'put on their clothes, not to be in danger of his heate' (p. 123). Although such passages are rare in the *Urania*, they are not likely to be found in male-written literature; they show both the author's occasional boldness in risking censure and her attempt to steer away from stereotypical treatment of female relationships.

In contrast to and conflicting with sixteenth-century gender ideology, the romance genre gave female characters more opportunities for sexual expression. Wroth makes use of these opportunities as far as she can do. Her women show a considerable degree of sexual responsiveness (pp. 104, 172), while they also possess relative autonomy and freedom in geographical movement.[42] Earlier chivalresque romances had restricted the principal female characters by confining them indoors. (We might recall the *Mirrour*'s Briana and Olivia, who wait at home for their lovers' return and who use messengers to communicate with the outside world.) Following the conventions of the pastoral romance, Wroth lets her female characters travel in open space, but she often breaks the conventions by letting them wander off independently, without men's guidance and protection. In this way the author also helps to bridge the gap between male and female experiences.

Indeed, Wroth makes a substantial contribution to women in literature by refuting traditional divisions of experience. Male-written romances had countered conventional associations of experience (arms, sports, and weighty conversation with men; indoor activities, beauty, and light conversation with women) by presenting the amazon type. But Wroth opposes the stereotype with much more realistic female characters. The lady that Dolorindus falls in love with is 'more then woman-like excellent in riding,' a subject about which, to her surprise, he is ignorant. And she is likewise able 'to discourse of martiall things, being excellently learned in all the Arts, knowledge no way scanting her' (pp. 153, 154). Another lady, Lysia, is equally skilful in traditionally male sports: 'The Lady was great, and therefore fair, full of spirit, and intising, pleasing and richly she was attired, and bravely served, an excellent hunts-woman she was, though these be no properer commendations, as some have said, than to say, a man is a fine Sempster, or Needle-man' (p. 470). The language of these passages, and the fact that in them women are juxtaposed to not so 'masculine' men, suggest

Wroth's awareness of her culture's division of experience. Unlike Sidney in the *Arcadia*, his niece in the *Urania* shows that interesting women are not necessarily those who possess beauty and virtue alone.

Wroth also challenges traditional divisions of experience by showing that the writing of poetry is not just a male preoccupation. Although the image of the woman writing love poems was not new in Renaissance literature (Shakespeare's Rosalind in *As You Like It* comes readily to mind), in the *Urania* it is given a more serious and realistic treatment. There are more women than men writing poems in Wroth's book, and it is shown that the writing of poetry is a talent or skill that can characterize a woman as much as anything else can. Poetic expression constitutes part of Pamphilia's identity.

The traps of defence and the struggle for a way out

If, as her contemporaries thought, Mary Wroth was 'dancing in a net,' it was a net of their making, not of hers. Indeed, her work as a whole suggests to us that she is greatly restricted by gender notions prevalent in her culture. Like many other women writers analysed in this study, however, Mary Wroth does not rebel against restrictive ideologies. Her affair with Pembroke and the two illegitimate children she bore him might suggest that in her personal life she sometimes defied convention and public opinion. Yet in her literary work she does not take such liberties. Arguably, she could have but did not. Nevertheless, there were many obstacles, mostly outside her control. Like her predecessors, Wroth was limited by first, the need to establish a respectable and credible voice; second, the centuries-long accusations against women; and third, the lack of appropriate language for an effective refutation or counter-position. Wroth adopts the vocabulary that equates masculine with strong and feminine with weak because she cannot invent new terms. History and tradition up to that time had offered few examples, if any, of critical discourse that challenges the assumptions of the roles and attributes assigned to the two sexes since classical times. These factors force Wroth into a largely defensive posture (of proving that women are not what they have been accused of being) and limit the ground of her search for solutions. Like other women writers, Wroth does not propose new models but criticizes from a position within the established ideology. Like them, too, she carries out her criticism by utilizing and modifying rather than rejecting conventional ideals and models.

Yet Mary Wroth's attempt to search for solutions within the traditional scheme of romantic love and marriage, in conjunction with her adoption of a defensive stand, inevitably and unfortunately lands her into contradictions and impasses. This situation creates a tension more apparent in the *Urania* than in the works of other Renaissance Englishwomen. The text discloses that while she refutes one stereotype through conventional means, she inadvertently runs into situations as undesirable for women as the stereotype she so persistently tries to refute; while she attempts to solve one problem she falls into another, or becomes trapped in the solution she proposes.

To establish a credible voice, Wroth utilizes conventionally respectable characters. In the *Urania* she may present more realistic versions of the amazon type, but unconventional attributes are usually relegated to minor or incidental characters. Her heroines are overall conventional women,[43] and it is partly because of this that they can be taken seriously. Here and there Wroth has to modify or liberalize established rules of feminine conduct, but the basic terms of negotiation are those of her culture. This is apparent in many instances. The standard of 'virtue' is not altogether rejected but adjusted to serve specific needs. Sensitive to the situation of the unhappily married woman,[44] Wroth justifies adultery when it is the result of oppression on the part of husbands or fathers, yet the adulterous woman must still be presented as 'virtuous' if she is to elicit the reader's sympathy and respect. The result is a narrowing of the concept of virtue to mean almost solely absence of sexual intercourse. Limena, a sympathetically portrayed adulteress who is killed by her 'brutish' and jealous husband, happily accepts her lover's (Perissus's) kisses but bids him not to 'dispose otherwise then virtuously of me' (p. 7). The same meaning of virtue is noticed in the stories of Curiardinus (p. 472) and Parselius (p. 105). Likewise, conventional rules regarding feminine conduct, speech, and dress are deployed, especially in cases where the woman's respectability is in need of defence. Another adulteress who is presented as a betrayed victim (pp. 350–1) is described as 'faire of complexion, good eyes, and of so modest a behaviour, as if her own tongue had not accused her, she had passed unblam'd for any show or ill in her fashion, or lightnesse in countenance' (p. 351). Limena, mentioned above, is 'able and sufficient to judge, or advise in any matter we could discourse of: but modestie in her caus'd it, onely loving knowledge, to be able to discern mens understandings by their arguments, but no way to shew it by her owne speech' (p. 7).

Although Wroth often describes the distressing position of the woman who cannot show her romantic interest in a man before he declares his (Pamphilia's case at the beginning), none the less she does not and cannot allow women to appear sexually aggressive. Orilena 'blushed to see she had [unwittingly] first told her tale' (p. 172). Taking the first step is clearly the man's role in the *Urania* as well as in the author's culture (and arguably in our own). The most Wroth can do is let the woman take the man's hand when he offers it to her. In the following scene between two lovers, Dalinea and Parselius, the author stretches the woman's acceptable sexual conduct to its very limits. Notice the distinction between male 'bashfulness' and 'woman modestie':

> She found it [his hand], and understood what hee would have her understand, nay, shee would answer his lookes with as amorous ones of her part, as staightly, and lovingly would she hold his hand, but knowing modesty forbid, shee would sigh, and in her soule wish that he would once speake; but bashfulnesse with-held him and woman modestie kept her silent.
>
> (pp. 103–4)

The heroine Pamphilia, Wroth's ideal female, is a very skilful versifier and an independent woman who walks alone in solitary places, refusing the escorting service of the man who courts her (p. 178). But she is also 'spotless' in her conduct, reticent, silent, secretive, and self-controlled.

The last of these attibutes, self-control, is in fact a very important one for Wroth and its treatment shows the kind of difficulty the author runs into with the conventional ideology she employs. Although Wroth sympathizes with women who experience jealous despair from disappointment in love (Antissia, Liana, Nereana), she shows no tolerance for hysterical behaviour, or what she calls 'over-weening' and 'lunatick ac-tions' (p. 291). Wroth apparently disliked ill-tempered behaviour in both men and women. When she attacked Denny she accused him of 'drunkenness' and lack of self-control. But the author's attitude in this matter is probably also influenced by the stereotype of the overreacting woman inherited from Ovid and other classical writers. Like Whitney before her, Wroth refutes this stereotype, which in any case conflicts with her thesis that women are the constant sex,[45] but her refutation inadvertently pushes her closer to her culture's ideal of the patient, silent, and self-controlled female. That is, Wroth counters the stereotype not by challenging the assumptions behind it but by finally falling back on the restrictions inherent in and imposed by her culture and from which she at times tries to escape. This is even more obvious in Wroth's treatment of constancy, the central subject of her book.

In scores of mirroring episodes throughout the *Urania*, Wroth shows how men change their affections and partners, sometimes against their better judgement. Approximately two-thirds into the book she even states, through one of her female characters, that men's inconstancy is due to 'their naturall infirmitie, and cannot be helped' (p. 375). Having done so, she does not drop the subject. She tries instead to elaborate on the problems that male unfaithfulness causes women. And rather than propose that women treat men in the same fashion, she tries to maintain the cultural ideal of female constancy even in the face of male changeableness. By the end of the book, most of the major female characters marry either their first loves or, if these proved fickle, their second, more faithful ones, and live happily ever after. But Wroth is not satisfied with this solution which would prove only that women are as inconstant as men. So she gives a battle for constancy. Her heroine Pamphilia and certain minor female characters who mirror her condition persist in remaining faithful to their first loves long after the latter have proven unsteadfast in their affections. Through these characters, but especially through her heroine, Wroth tries to negotiate and uphold the cultural ideal of female constancy. What becomes evident in the process is that she cannot do so without sacrificing the woman's personal freedom. In the course of proving her constancy, Pamphilia loses her sense of self and becomes a passive, subjugated woman.

In the *Urania* Wroth assigns two major roles to Pamphilia, that of queen (of the kingdom of Pamphilia) and constant lover (of the changing Amphilanthus, king of Naples). Yet the author does not make her heroine play out her two roles equally. This may be partly due to the lack of proper models. Elizabeth I could wield political power by pitting one man against the other in the competition for her favour and by giving up marriage. Garnier's *Antonie*, which Lady Mary's aunt had translated for the English public, had showed the disastrous results of Cleopatra's attempt to live out both roles. The romance genre itself had withheld from heroines active roles and ambitious preoccupations. So Wroth had no precedents that could teach her how to reconcile a woman's strong passion for a man, her culture's ideal of constancy, and her political position. The problem of models is further complicated by the fact that Wroth's interest lies primarily outside politics. Unlike her uncle who in his *Arcadia* dealt with many of the political issues that confronted the Elizabethan administration, Wroth focuses on love and human relationships, thus breaking away from the chivalric tradition and anticipating the concerns of later novelists. As a result of all this, Pamphilia the lover predominates and Pamphilia the queen becomes politically unambitious. Although like Queen Elizabeth she states that she is married to her kingdom 'from which Husband shee could not bee divorced, nor ever would have other' (p. 218),[46] such a declaration is made by way of eluding her father's suggestion that she marry Leandrus, one of the men who court her. The real reason, which she finally confesses to her father, is that she cannot love Leandrus (p. 218). In a moment of self-reflection, Pamphilia recognizes that her love has incapacitated her as a political figure: 'Poore people, how are you deceived, that thinke your Queene is here? alas tis nothing so, shee is farre off, it may be in the field performing famous acts, it may be on the Sea passing to fetch more fame, or indeed speaking with thy selfe, as I discourse to him' (p. 265). Sadly, Pamphilia here experiences only mentally the type of action she could be participating in on account of her position as queen. Like many other faithful women in the *Urania*, Pamphilia becomes debilitated, consuming nearly all her time and energy in lamenting the absence of her lover or his desertion of her. His inconstancy causes her a great deal of pain, but she would rather endure pain than give up her constancy:

Deceived I am; yet why didst thou plot for my ruine? . . .
Yet Amphilanthus true or false, I must still love thee best,
and though thou wrong me, I must love thee still. What
torments have I alas for thee indurd?

(p. 252)

Ready to forgive his transgression, she invites him to come
back, offering herself 'at thy feet . . . thy vassall' (p. 252). As the
wording here and elsewhere suggests, Wroth is aware of what
has happened to her heroine: Pamphilia has lost her energy
and sense of self and has given in to passivity, subjugation,
and humiliation. Unlike the lover of the medieval court lady,
Amphilanthus has become her master, not her servant. But
neither Pamphilia nor her creator is willing to give up the
struggle, which becomes articulated in a significant and long
conversation between Pamphilia and her close friend and
confidante, Urania. When Pamphilia remarks that a change of
scene cannot 'aspire' to alter her mood or attitude towards love,
Urania warns her that prizing constancy as a virtue in itself can
lead to single-mindedness:

Change (said Urania) deserves no honour; but discretion
may make you discerne when you should bee constant,
and when discreete, and thus you doe not change but
continue, judiciall as alwayes you have beene.

(p. 391)

In any case, Urania argues when the two continue the discussion
later, giving excessive importance to love is a weakness, not a
strength:

I love Love, as he should be loved, and so deare Lady do
you, and then you will plainly see, he is not such a Deity,
as your Idolatry makes him, but a good child well use
flattred [sic], an insolent thing comming over our harts,
as children over the poore birds they catch before they can
flie, thinking they master them, when indeede it is their
want of wings makes their bondage; and so deare Cosin it
is our want of courage and judgement makes us his slaves.

(p. 399)[47]

When Pamphilia insists, 'so well hath love instructed me, as I
can never leave my master nor his precepts' (p. 400), her friend

reminds her of the danger in holding as absolute values which are likely to change with time:

> Tis pitie said Urania, that ever that fruitlesse thing Constancy was taught you as a vertue, since for vertues sake you will love it, as having true possession of your soule, but understand, this vertue hath limits to hold it in, being a vertue, but thus that it is a vice in them that breake it, but those with whom it is broken, are by the breach free to leave or choose againe where more staidnes may be found; besides tis a dangerous thing to hold that opinion, which in time will prove flat heresie.
>
> (p. 400)

Such passages show both the author's psychological insight into the effects on the female mind of notions like constancy, and her awareness that the value of such notions is culturally produced and therefore not permanent. Furthermore, the fact that these passages are spoken by Urania gives them force and credibility. Next to Pamphilia, Urania is probably the author's highest prized character. Not only does she bear the name of the book, which opens with a description of her search for her lost identity, but later on she is upheld as one of the two models for admiration. In the Palace of Love, where all the lovers gather to test their constancy, she shares the throne with Pamphilia, both 'beheld by the rest, as fittest to be admired' (p. 355). Wroth's Urania does not exercise any celestial kind of influence over people, as her namesake does in the opening scene of Sidney's *Arcadia*; instead, she aims to influence by offering sensible advice. What especially qualifies her as a counsellor is the fact that she has achieved her goal of finding her lost identity (as the missing sister of Amphilanthus), and has been able to maintain a healthy balance in her love relationships with men. Her conventionally admirable conduct and the associations of her name[48] with divine contemplation are additional qualifications for a credible speaker.

However, it is significant that Pamphilia is not convinced by Urania, and apparently neither is the author. The heroine's problem is also her creator's. Wroth is not a detached observer on the subject but deeply implicated in the conflict she depicts. Despite the fact that she can see the woman's high personal costs of maintaining constancy in a changing world, and despite the fact also that she presents a forceful and well-qualified advocate against meaningless constancy, she is still ambivalent and waivers between a Pamphilia and a Urania. This ambivalence does not appear to be resolved in the published *Urania*, which ends with a feeling that the Pamphilia–Amphilanthus relationship repeats the same pattern of desertion and return; the last word in the book is 'and.' Nor is the ambivalence actually resolved in the sonnet sequence *Pamphilia to Amphilanthus*, which Wroth revised, rearranged, and appended to the 1621 printed *Urania*.[49] Ambivalent feelings about constancy occur throughout the four sections of the sequence, in which Wroth dramatizes the conflict between 'passionate surrender and self affirmation.'[50] At the very end of the sequence a 'fragile hope,' in Roberts's phrase, emerges, but the conflict remains largely unresolved despite the attempted final shift of focus from earthly to heavenly love. That Wroth did not consider the matter settled is evident above all from the fact that she wrote a second part to the *Urania*, which remains in manuscript form at the Newbury Library. At the end of this second part, Roberts reports, Pamphilia 'comes to recognize the impossibility of maintaining perfect constancy in a world of human frailty'[51] and, abandoning her love for Amphilanthus, finally marries someone else (the king of Tartary). But so much preoccupation with the subject[52] suggests the author's difficulty in finally rejecting the cultural ideal and leaving women exposed to criticism. It also suggests how strong a grip the idea of romantic love had on the author. Yet one thing is certain: Wroth does not treat romantic love as though it were a private matter, separate from culture. She accepts its general premises and works within them at the same time that she shows the problem it poses for women in a culture which practises a double standard and holds up for admiration the woman who will endorse this standard by remaining faithful to an inconstant man. The critique Wroth offers and the problems she points to are no different from those in modern-day romances.[53] Wroth does not propose any solutions in the published *Urania*. Throughout the book she suggests various possibilities (such as those represented by Urania and Silviana) but does not seem to put forward any of these with conviction. She remains uncertain until the end of her book.

There is some evidence to suggest that part of this uncertainty

5

CONCLUSION

Dominant ideologies in the Renaissance oppressed women with their theories of female inferiority and male superiority. Women had no legal rights, no public voice, and certainly no literary voice (outside the accepted areas of religion and domesticity). But like all ideologies, these in the Renaissance were not monolithic. Contradictions within them, inefficient surveillance (too much or not enough control), and the unforeseen course of change itself left room for subordinate groups like women to manoeuvre their way through. With these premises, I have tried to analyse the secular writings of a number of Renaissance Englishwomen. My aim has been principally to explore their opposition to prevailing cultural norms and ideologies and to identify the various writing strategies they employ, considering all along their subjectivity as women in a culture inimical to female creative activity.

As in the case of later women writers, opposition to dominant ideologies is found primarily in the area of gender. With very few exceptions, notably Mary Herbert's *Antonie* (a translated text) and Elizabeth Cary's *Edward II* (an original draft of a play), which deal with problems of statecraft as well as gender, women write about and criticize their relationship to men in particular and to patriarchy in general. Isabella Whitney refutes Ovidian and other stereotypes of women as fickle and hysterical; Mary Herbert indirectly counters the stereotype of woman as whore and seductress by translating a play about a sexually untainted Cleopatra; and Mary Wroth exposes the binds that women are placed in by tyrannical fathers on the one hand and inconstant lovers on the other.

Opposition to established ideas in these areas is usually

circumscribed. At times the writers openly challenge certain oppressive notions. Tyler, for example, directly confronts and refutes the assumptions and rules which bar women's entrance to traditionally male literary genres; and Wroth quarrels with Lord Denny publicly on equal terms, requiring him to observe rules of decent conduct and refusing to accept his distinctions of feminine and masculine. Yet neither these nor any of the other women in the group I consider actually advocate a complete departure from the established order of sexual and social relationships, and seldom do they attack basic assumptions in the ideologies that oppress them. Rarely, if at all, for instance, is the requirement of feminine sexual modesty either flouted or seriously questioned. The women authors I have studied do not actually propose radical alternatives. While they criticize the existing relation between the two sexes, they aim to reinscribe or resituate themselves within the established order. Wroth, for instance, criticizes fathers, husbands, and lovers for their tyranny, jealousy, and inconstancy respectively, but she does not attack the basic structure of the institution of marriage. In fact, as I have tried to show, she insists on searching for solutions within the traditional scheme of romantic love and marriage, despite her own awareness that there are serious problems in that area.

This attempt to claim a better, less oppressive position within traditional structures rather than to seek to challenge their basis on new terms is largely due to the discursive impasse these women often face. Strongly influenced by the long history of accusations against the female sex, they frequently adopt a defensive speaking position which entraps them in different types of oppression from the ones they contest. This is evident in several of the works I have examined, but it is particularly apparent in Wroth's *Urania* and sonnet sequence. Through various characters, Wroth proves time and again that women are the constant sex, contrary to male allegations. But in remaining faithful to her inconstant lover, her heroine Pamphilia loses her emotional independence and sense of self.

The discursive impasse is also a factor of language. The absence of a linguistic idiom that could both express women's desires and serve as a medium of effective criticism of dominant ideology is a great obstacle. The critique of male/female relations is carried out in the moral terms already established by discourses such as the *querrelle de femmes*, the debate on the nature of women. Socio-economic matters are very rarely considered. Sometimes remaining within conventional territory or toning down the oppositional voice seems to be a consciously deployed textual strategy, dictated by the author's purpose in writing. It is very difficult, and often impossible, however, to say with certainty when a particular author is consciously using this as a method. Usually, there is tension and ambiguity. Lanyer is a case in point. She apparently aims to profit from writing and dedicates her book to women only. In her work, which combines feminism with religion, the defence of women appears to be not only a way of contesting oppression but also a strategy for soliciting financial support from her female dedicatees. But tension is present in the text and several threads intertwine.

Although, as I have noted, these women at times directly challenge oppressive notions and practices in their culture, more often they voice their critique by employing, consciously or unconsciously, strategies of appropriation, accommodation, and modification. Usually not one but a combination of these work within the same text. Appropriation usually involves the use of conventional ideas, language, or rules of conduct to achieve a desired end. Motherly care or sexual modesty, for example, are appropriated by several authors to justify a female character's transgressive actions (e.g. adultery or disobedience) and to render the character sympathetic to the audience. Also, conventional virtues in a woman are often used to legitimate that woman's dissenting views: the woman is a paragon, has everything convention could ask for, but she disagrees on certain things. Sometimes appropriation involves appeal to an ideal higher than the one practised in contemporary culture. The ideals of marriage for love and virtuous constancy for both sexes become the premises of a critique of lovers, husbands, and fathers. Accommodation usually works as an attempt to reconcile contradictory desires or principles. Cary tries to accommodate her own internalization of feminine propriety and her desire to act independently. But the result is not necessarily a harmonious union. Cary's heroines evince a rift between wifely duty and insubordination. The strategy of modification permits the authors to adapt conventional language to their purposes. Wroth, for example, narrows the meaning of the term 'virtue' to absence of sexual intercourse. These strategies are present as well in the male-authored literary texts which Englishwomen translate; these texts may be called 'feminine' in their style and the position they adopt *vis-à-vis* dominant ideology.

The women I discuss employ such strategies also to validate their position as authors (i.e. to enter the literary field). Isabella Whitney legitimates her writing activity by endorsing and slightly modifying conventional ideas regarding proper female occupations; writing books becomes something to do while waiting for a husband and household duties. And Elizabeth Cary claims her right to offer her own version of *Edward II* by appropriating the notion of absolute truth; she writes 'to please the Truth, not Time.'

As I discuss earlier, the strategies these women use to express opposition as writers frequently combine with strategies for other purposes, such as negotiating economic and class restrictions. Women who write for profit (Whitney and Lanyer most probably belong to this category) face both the problems of the male professional writer and those of the woman writing in a culture which considers her intellectually inferior to man and forbids her to compete with him.

Accordingly, they employ strategies which can work to their advantage. Whitney counters cultural stereotypes of women at the same time that she establishes authorial credibility by echoing conduct-book dicta. Lanyer attacks men's presumptuousness but introduces herself as 'wife to Captain Alfonso Lanyer, Servant to the Kings Majestie,' and chooses to versify a religious and hence respectable story.

The issue of class recurs. In the case of middle-class women, especially those adopting the position of the male professional writer, social rank becomes a barrier to patronage and to addressing an aristocratic audience. One woman, Aemilia Lanyer, in the group of six I discuss, makes an obvious attempt to attract patrons. But her choice of subject matter, her negotiating manoeuvres, and her selection of dedicatees (noblewomen of her acquaintance) evince the limitations posed by her social position. In the case of aristocratic women writers, high social standing worked to their disadvantage as cultural gender notions combined with court or family influence to suppress their work. Both Lady Mary Wroth and Lady Elizabeth Cary had to withdraw their published books from circulation. Class also becomes a line of demarcation between groups of these writers.

Only Wroth seems to escape strict classification displaying the characteristics of a woman between classes. Lady Elizabeth Cary and Lady Mary Herbert, who share a lot between them, are very far removed from the spirit of women like Whitney and Tyler. Cary and Herbert seem more indirect and more hesitant to violate feminine decorum. This is nowhere more apparent than in their reluctance to appear in print, although they were anxious to write. The strongest, most direct opposition comes mainly from women of the middle classes.

Differences among authors are noticed mainly in the degree of directness and consciousness. Tyler, Whitney, and Lanyer are much more vocal and forthright than Cary and Herbert. This, as I mention above, is partly due to class. Women of the upper ranks were usually subject to greater restrictions than women of the middle or lower ranks. Differences in the degree of consciousness are less easily identifiable. Some of the women authors show internalization of the ideologies that oppressed them; others seem aware of the cultural construction of these ideologies and the disadvantageous position of women. Most of them display an amazing awareness of the charges against the female sex and the uneven distribution of power between the two sexes in society. Thus, though these writers cannot be called feminists in the sense of offering a coherent ideology of women as an oppressed group, they can be said to possess a feminist spirit in recognizing the limitations imposed on women and in attempting, however indirectly at times, to combat these limitations. What all of them also appear to have in common are valuable skills which helped them to overcome cultural obstacles – ingenuity and critical discernment, in addition to poetic talent. All six of them are individuals who sought to come to terms with the conflict between desire and oppression. Such attributes, viewed alongside the writing strategies these women employ, attest to the narrowness of available space and means.

In the process of reading the texts, I was not specifically looking for signs of 'progress,' but certain conclusions can be drawn in relation to chronology. The oppositional voice does not necessarily get louder with time. Between about 1570 and 1630 one can hardly speak of a linear development either in the degree of feminist consciousness or in the kind of resistance to oppressive ideas. Mary Wroth's critique is not radically different from Whitney's, though it is more incisive. But the circumstances and the spirit of the criticism do change, showing Jacobean women more confident and assertive. The fact that a woman like Mary Wroth can satirize her class and engage in public polemics with a powerful lord is indeed quite significant. One cannot imagine such an event taking place much before the turn of the sixteenth century. This study has suggested that the period of the late Renaissance as a whole has to be treated as a historical moment to be compared to earlier and later periods. For if the contrast between Wroth and Whitney is not great, there is a great difference between Wroth and, say, Margaret Roper, at least as far as the public image is concerned.

Like any study, the present one has its limitations. Perhaps the greatest limitation concerns the paucity of evidence, both historical and biographical. This has made it virtually impossible to explore the very interesting relationship between women's lives and their ideas in writing. Only in the cases of Elizabeth Cary and Mary Herbert has it been relatively possible to do so, for the women I write about left very few pieces of autobiographical evidence (letters, diaries, etc.). The development in a woman writer's work is often very important as it can tell us more about the process of cultural negotiation, yet in the case of Renaissance women authors we do not have the option of tracing such development. With the possible exception of Elizabeth Cary, we know very little about their later experiences and how these may have changed their views or confirmed them. We hear a tantalizing bit of information, and then many years elapse before we hear anything further in connection with the same author. This lack of information has forced me to speculate even on such important issues as the suppression of a book. The conclusions of this study, therefore, must remain tentative until more evidence is found to corroborate or modify whatever claims are made here. Yet, whatever its limitations, I hope this study provides a detailed and honest reading of the texts, which until recently had been ignored – indeed, many are still unavailable. Recent feminist scholars have made efforts to redress the situation by editing some of Renaissance women's writings, but much still remains to be done in providing the modern reader with the necessary texts.

NOTES

1 CULTURE, CHANGE, AND WOMEN'S RESPONSES

1 Some of the research published in the field in recent years includes: Margaret Ferguson *et al.* (eds), *Rewriting the Renaissance: The Discourses of Sexual Difference in Early Modern Europe* (Chicago: University of Chicago Press, 1986); Josephine Roberts (ed.), *The Poems of Lady Mary Wroth* (Baton Rouge: Louisiana University Press, 1983); Margaret Hannay (ed.), *Silent But for the Word: Tudor Women as Patrons, Translators and Writers of Religious Works* (Kent, Ohio: Kent State University Press, 1986); Mary Beth Rose (ed.), *Women in the Middle Ages and the Renaissance: Literary and Historical Perspectives* (Syracuse: Syracuse University Press, 1986); Katharina Wilson, *Women Writers of the English Renaissance and Reformation* (Athens: University of Georgia Press, 1987); Ann Haselkorn and Betty Travitsky (eds), *The Renaissance Englishwoman in Print, 1500–1640* (Amherst, Massachusetts: University of Massachusetts Press, 1990); and Ann Rosalind Jones, *The Currency of Eros: Women's Love Lyric in Europe, 1540–1620* (Bloomington: Indiana University Press, 1990).

2 V. Woolf, *A Room Of One's Own* (London: Panther Books, 1977), p. 41.

3 Alan Sinfield discusses this concept in his essay, 'Power and ideology: an outline theory and Sidney's *Arcadia*,' *English Literary History*, 52 (1985), esp. pp. 265–9.

4 Michel Foucault, *Power/Knowledge: Selected Interviews and Other Writings 1972–1977*, ed. C. Gordon (Brighton: Harvester Press, 1980), p. 142.

5 In R. Bridenthal and C. Koonz (eds), *Becoming Visible: Women in European History* (Boston: Houghton Mifflin, 1977).

6 M. Ferguson *et al.* (eds), *Rewriting the Renaissance*, pp. xxx–xxxi.

7 Jacob Burckhardt, *The Civilization of the Renaissance in Italy* (1860), trans. S. Middlemore (New York: Albert and Charles Boni, 1935), p. 389.

8 Mary Ellen Lamb, 'The Cooke sisters: attitudes toward learned women in the Renaissance,' in M. Hannay (ed.), *Silent But for the Word*, pp. 107–25.

9　Judith Brown, 'A woman's place was in the home: women's work in Renaissance Tuscany,' in M. Ferguson *et al.* (eds), *Rewriting the Renaissance*, p. 222.

10　Recent studies have questioned the universality of this effect as well as the conclusions of Clark's pioneer study, *The Working Life of Women in the Seventeenth Century*. It has been suggested that until the advent of the factory system much small-scale production was still carried out in the home. Clark's evidence contradicts her thesis. See Judith Brown, cited above.

11　Keith Wrightson and Alan Macfarlane assert with evidence that the family structure and forms of behaviour Stone claims for the companionate family of the late seventeenth and early eighteenth centuries were already the norm throughout most of the sixteenth. Though they accept Stone's conclusions about the aristocracy, they criticize him for applying aristocratic tendencies to the rest (and greatest) part of the population. (See K. Wrightson, *English Society 1580–1680* (New Jersey: Rutgers University Press, 1982); A. Macfarlane, *The Origins of English Individualism* (Oxford: Basil Blackwell, 1978); and L. Stone, *The Family, Sex and Marriage* (London: Weidenfeld & Nicolson, 1977).)

12　Louis B. Wright, *Middle-Class Culture in Elizabethan England* (London: Methuen, 1935), p. 207.

13　L. Stone, op. cit., p. 154.

14　Quoted in R. Kelso, *Doctrine for the Lady of the Renaissance* (Urbana: University of Illinois Press, 1956), p. 51.

15　Quoted by Valerie Wayne in M. Hannay (ed.), *Silent But for the Word*, p. 23.

16　Elizabeth F. Rogers, *St. Thomas More: Selected Letters* (New Haven and London: Yale University Press, 1961), p. 155.

17　Gordon Schochet, *Patriarchalism and Political Thought* (Oxford: Blackwell, 1975), *passim*; Peter Stallybrass, 'The body enclosed: patriarchal territories,' in M. Ferguson *et al.* (eds), *Rewriting the Renaissance*, pp. 130–1. The principles of patriarchy were expounded in 1576 by Jean Bodin in *Six Livres de la République*, but patriarchal ideas had circulated earlier. In the seventeenth century Robert Filmer published his *Patriarcha: A Defense of the Natural Power of Kings against the Unnatural Liberty of the People*.

18　In his book *The First Blast of the Trumpet Against the Monstruous Regiment of Women*, published in Geneva in 1558, Knox asserted, using biblical evidence, the God-given superiority of Adam over Eve and argued that women were not created to rule, for they were by nature weak, frail, impatient, and feeble.

19　Cited by Ann Jones in 'Nets and Bridles,' in N. Armstrong and L. Tennenhouse (eds), *The Ideology of Conduct: Female Courtesy Books and Literature From the Middle Ages to the Present Day* (London: Methuen, 1987), p. 53.

20　ibid, p. 61.

21　Suzanne Hull, *Chaste, Silent and Obedient* (San Marino: Huntington Library, 1982), p. 134.

22 R. Kelso, op. cit. p. 83.
23 S. Hull, op. cit., p. 52; R. Kelso, op. cit., p. 91.
24 R. Kelso, op. cit., p. 91.
25 K. Wrightson, p. 92.
26 'The Changing Family,' *The Times Literary Supplement*, 21 October 1977, p. 1226.
27 Cited by S. Hull, op. cit., p. 73.
28 Retha Warnicke, *Women of the English Renaissance and Reformation* (Westport, Connecticut: Greenwood Press, 1983), p. 56.
29 Natalie Zemon Davies, *Society and Culture in Early Modern France* (London: Duckworth, 1975), p. 84.
30 Lisa Jardine, *Still Harping on Daughters: Women and Drama in the Age of Shakespeare* (Totowa, N.J.: Barnes & Noble, 1983), p. 51.
31 R. Warnicke, op. cit., p. 56; Hugh Latimer, *Selected Sermons*, ed. Allan G. Stester (Charlottesville, Virginia: University of Virginia Press, 1968), p. 153.
32 Cited in Dorothy Gardiner, *English Girlhood at School* (Oxford: Oxford University Press, 1929), p. 196.
33 We do not know, however, whether women were different from men in publishing predominantly religious works. A tabulation of the male output in the two subject categories, religious and secular, is not currently available.
34 Cited in Patricia Labalme (ed.), *Beyond Their Sex: Learned Women of the European Past* (New York: New York University Press, 1980), p. 118.
35 Elaine Beilin, 'Anne Askew's self-portait in the *Examinations*,' in M. Hannay (ed.), *Silent But for the Word*, p. 90.
36 Natalie Zemon Davies shows that Weber was wrong in saying that women were attracted to religion because they found it inciting to orgy and emotion (*Society and Culture in Early Modern France*, p. 79). For a well-documented and interesting discussion of the subject see the critical appendices of the recent *Biographical Dictionary of English Women Writers 1580–1720*, ed. Maureen Bell *et al.* (Brighton: Harvester, 1990).
37 Keith Thomas, 'Women and the Civil War sects,' in T. Aston (ed.), *Crisis in Europe 1560–1660* (London: Routledge & Kegan Paul, 1965), p. 320.
38 R. Warnicke, op. cit., p. 146.
39 K. Thomas, 'Women and the Civil War sects,' p. 328.
40 ibid., pp. 338, 340.
41 Ann Jones, 'Nets and bridles,' p. 40; Ian McLean, *The Renaissance Notion of Woman* (Cambridge: Cambridge University Press, 1980), pp. 1, 24–7.
42 Lisa Jardine, 'Cultural confusion and Shakespeare's learned heroines,' *Shakespeare Quarterly*, 38 (Spring 1987), pp. 1–18.
43 Retha Warnicke suggests that the early humanists failed to popularize their theories on women's classical education in part because their female models (Catherine of Aragon, the More

daughters, and Princess Mary) became unfashionable after More's execution (*Women of the English Renaissance and Reformation*, p. 91). I believe they failed also because their programme (the study of Greek and Latin specifically) did not sufficiently address the larger needs of the English aristocracy.

44 Quoted in David Cressy, *Education in Tudor and Stuart England* (London: Edward Arnold, 1975), p. 5.

45 R. Kelso, op. cit., pp. 59–60.

46 Historians differ in their estimates of literacy figures because firm evidence is lacking. According to David Cressy, only about 5 per cent of Englishwomen could sign their names during the sixteenth and most of the seventeenth centuries (*Literacy and Social Order*, pp. 145–7). But Cressy bases his conclusions on court depositions alone and leaves women socially undifferentiated. Suzanne Hull, who surveys Renaissance books for women, implies a much higher literacy rate. She shows that in the last quarter of the sixteenth century, women emerge as a distinct reading group (*Chaste, Silent and Obedient*, pp. 9–13). Most historians recognize that reading and writing rates must be separated, seeing reading as a much more socially diffused skill (Margaret Spufford, *Small Books and Pleasant Histories . . .*, p. 27; H.S. Bennett, *English Books and Readers, 1603–1640*, pp. 85–6; S. Hull, op. cit., p. 4). Where women learned to read and write is a question that has puzzled historians. It appears that the petty schools provided one means. Wrightson states that in the second half of the sixteenth century there was a proliferation of these elementary schools, which taught literacy skills to local children (*English Society 1580–1680*, p. 185). Another means was provided by itinerant freelance teachers. According to Cressy, the importance of these teachers is much greater than their shadowy appearance in records indicates (*Education in Tudor and Stuart England*, p. 36). Informal teaching by relatives or neighbours is suggested by the popularity of self-instruction guides like *The English Schoolmaster* (J.W. Adamson, 'The extent of literacy in England,' *The Library*, 10 (1930), p. 187).

47 Lawrence Stone, 'The educational revolution in England 1560–1640,' *Past and Present*, 28 (1964), pp. 41–80.

48 Some grammar schools did admit girls, as can be inferred from the provisos in the statutes of these schools. See J.W. Adamson, op. cit., pp. 189–93.

49 Louis B. Wright, 'The reading of Renaissance Englishwomen,' *Studies in Philology*, 28 (1931), pp. 139–57.

50 K. Wrightson, op. cit., p. 198.

51 Many of the ideas in this section are derived from Ann Jones's discussion of courtesy books in 'Nets and bridles,' already cited. I have also benefited greatly from the definition of courtiership she and Peter Stallybrass provide in their essay, 'The politics of *Astrophil and Stella*,' *Studies in English Literature*, 24 (1984), pp. 53–68.

52 D. Gardiner, op. cit., p. 114.

53 The prefatory material of the 1578 edition of *The Mirrour . . .* is

marked by signatures (A3–A6) rather than page numbers, which are used for the rest of the book.

54 Dedicatory epistle to *Mortalities Memorandum, with a Dreame Prefixed* (London: Edward Griffin for Jacob Bloome, 1621); reprinted in B. Travitsky (ed.), *The Paradise of Women: Writings by Englishwomen of the Renaissance* (Westport, Connecticut: Greenwood Press, 1981), p. 153.

55 Sandra Gilbert and Susan Gubar, *The Madwoman in the Attic: The Woman Writer and the Nineteenth-Century Literary Imagination* (New Haven: Yale University Press, 1979), p. 6.

56 ibid, p. 10.

57 See the correspondence of Mary Wroth appended by Josephine Roberts to her edition of *The Poems of Lady Mary Wroth*, cited above. See also my discussion on Mary Wroth later in this volume.

58 Gilbert and Gubar, op. cit., p. 50.

59 Joanna Russ, *How to Suppress Women's Writing* (London: The Women's Press, 1983), p. 87.

60 Linda Woodbridge states that the principal source of *exempla* used in the controversy was Boccaccio's *De Claris Mulieribus* (Concerning Famous Women), a collection of 104 brief biographies of women, gleaned mainly from Ovid. See L. Woodbridge, *Women and the English Renaissance* (Brighton: Harvester Press, 1984), p. 15.

61 Jones's excellent study, already cited, concentrates on women poets in France, Italy, and England. From the English side she includes Isabella Whitney and Lady Mary Wroth.

62 The Wilton group included, among others, Samuel Daniel, Ben Jonson, John Donne, and periodically Sir Philip Sidney. It also included one other woman, the Countess's cousin, Lady Harrington.

63 Lamb, 'The Cooke sisters,' p. 124.

64 ibid., p. 112.

65 Sir John Davies, *The Muses Sacrifice or Divine Meditations* (London: for G. Norton, 1612), sig. A1.

66 Hull offers some useful statistics on female patronage in the Renaissance: 1,780 books were dedicated to women, with 23 per cent of these to queens. Altogether some 800 different women received dedications in published books (*Chaste, Silent and Obedient*, pp. 18–24).

67 Mary Poovey makes a similar point about nineteenth-century writers in *The Proper Lady and the Woman Writer: Ideology as Style in the Works of Mary Wollstonecraft, Mary Shelley, and Jane Austen* (Chicago: University of Chicago Press, 1984), p. 43.

68 Jonathan Dollimore and Alan Sinfield (eds), *Political Shakespeare: New Essays in Cultural Materialism* (Manchester: Manchester University Press, 1985), p. 13.

69 Raymond Williams, *Marxism and Literature*, (Oxford: Oxford University Press, 1977), pp. 121–7.

70 Michele Barrett, 'Ideology and the cultural production of gender,' in Judith Newton and Deborah Rosenfelt (eds), *Feminist Criticism and*

Social Change: Sex, Class and Race in Literature and Culture, (New York and London: Methuen, 1985), p. 79. See also, Cora Kaplan, 'Radical feminism and literature: rethinking Millett's sexual politics,' *Red Letters*, 9 (1979), pp. 4–16.

2 SERVANT GIRLS CLAIMING MALE DOMAIN

1 See introduction to chapter three in this book for a discussion of the interrelation of class, gender ideology, and women's behaviour.
2 Isabella was the sister of Geoffrey Whitney, the Cheshire-born lawyer and writer of emblems (*A Choice of Emblemes*, 1586). This appears from a correlation between the will of Geoffry Whitney and the names of Isabella's brothers and sisters, as they are mentioned in her work. See Henry Green (ed.), *A Choice of Emblems* (London: Lovell Reeve, 1866, rpt. 1967); R.J. Fehrenbach, 'Isabella Whitney, Sir Hugh Plat, Geoffrey Whitney, and "Sister Eldershae,"' *English Language Notes*, September 1983; and the *DNB* entry for Whitney, Geoffrey. Isabella apparently came to London at an early age and subsequently kept contact with her country relatives and friends. It is quite likely that Isabella stayed with her brother for some time after she lost her position as servant and that he connected her with the publishing circles.
3 Betty Travitsky has published an edition of the 'Wyll and Testament' in *English Literary Renaissance*, 10.4 (1980), pp. 76–94. According to Travitsky, this poem is 'the most enduring of Isabella Whitney's writing.'
4 B. Travitsky (ed.), *The Paradise of Women: Writings by Englishwomen of the Renaissance* (Westport, Connecticut: Greenwood Press, 1981), p. 118.
5 I have used the British Library volume of *A Sweet Nosegay*, but for *The Copy of a Letter* I have relied on Richard Panofsky's facsimile edition, cited below (note 6).
6 Hugh Plat, entirely unknown as a poet, was the author of *The Floures of Philosophie* (1572), a series of Senecan *sententiae*, and of other books on science, gardening, and domestic management. Richard Panofsky has published, with an introduction, a facsimile edition of *The Floures of Philosophie (1572) by Hugh Plat and A Sweet Nosegay (1573) and The Copy of a Letter (1567) by Isabella Whitney* (Delmar, NY: Scholars' Facsimiles and Reprints, 1982).
7 Edwin Miller, *The Professional Writer in Elizabethan England: A Study of Nondramatic Literature* (Cambridge, Massachusetts: Harvard University Press, 1959), p. 150.
8 See R.J. Fehrenbach, 'Isabella Whitney and the Popular Miscellanies of Richard Jones,' *Cahiers Elizabéthains*, 19 (1981).
9 Betty Travitsky includes *The Copy of a Letter* in the corpus of feminist pamphlets (see 'The lady doth protest,' *English Literary Renaissance*, 14.3 (1984)) but Linda Woodbridge in *Women and the English Renaissance* (1984) does not. The poem differs from the later women-authored feminist tracts first in focusing on one

topic (men's deceptive behaviour) rather than on a point-by-point defence of women, and second in being written in verse rather than in prose.

10 *The Copy of a Letter* is written in the style of the Ovidian lament of the abandoned mistress, characterized by an exaggeration of grief. This style became popular after George Turberville's translation of Ovid's *Heroides* in 1567.

11 I am grateful to Ann Jones for initially calling my attention to Whitney's writing for a popular audience and its effect on style. Several of the ideas in my discussion of *The Copy of a Letter* will be found in Ann Jones's essay 'Nets and bridles', in N. Armstrong and L. Tennenhouse (eds), *The Ideology of Conduct* (London: Methuen, 1987) and in her interesting new book, *The Currency of Eros: Women's Love Lyric in Europe, 1540–1620* (Bloomington, Ind.: University of Indiana Press, 1990).

12 A. Jones, 'Nets and bridles,' p. 66.

13 B. Travitsky, 'The lady doth protest,' p. 262.

14 See my discussion of domestic service in the first chapter, and also R.J. Fehrenbach, 'A Letter sent by Maidens of London (1567),' *English Literary Renaissance*, 14.3 (1984), pp. 285–304.

15 Quoted by L.B. Wright in 'The reading of Renaissance, Englishwomen,' *Studies in Philology*, 28 (1931), p. 147. Among the prohibited romances, Vives lists *The Amandis, Celestina the Bawd, Lancelot du Lac, Paris and Vienne, Parthenope, Libius and Arthur, Guy,* and *Bevis.*

16 ibid., p. 141.

17 For a discussion of the possible reasons for women's attraction to the romance genre and its subversive character, see Tina Krontiris, 'Breaking barriers of genre and gender: Margaret Tyler's translation of the *Mirrour of Knighthood,*' *English Literary Renaissance*, 18.1 (1988), esp. pp. 23–8.

18 From the Dedication and the Preface, we understand that Tyler had been a servant in the household of the parents of Lord Howard. In her edition, *First Feminists: British Women Writers 1578–1799* (Bloomington: Indiana University Press, 1985), Moira Ferguson states that this was the Roman Catholic family of the Third Duke of Norfolk, who was executed in 1572. Ferguson also says there is a 'slim possibility' that Margaret Tyler's real name was Margaret Tyrrell, 'a prominent Roman Catholic family living at the time of the Howards' (p. 51). Tyler was probably of some age in 1578, for in her Preface she refers to writers of 'as aged years,' and to the reader's interpretation of 'my name and years.'

19 The title page of the earliest known edition of Tyler's translation reads as follows: *The Mirrour of Princely deedes and Knighthood: Wherein is shewed the worthinesse of the Knight of the Sunne, and his brother Rosicleer, sonnes to the great Emperour Trebatio: with the strange love of the beautifull and excellent Princesse Briana, and the valiant actes of other noble Princes and Knightes. Now newly translated out of Spanish into our vulgar English tongue, by M.T. Imprinted at London by Thomas East.* The copy is undated, but it is believed to

be the one licensed by the Stationer's company on 4 August 1578, STC 18859. It probably did not come out until 1580. For evidence of dating see J. Perott, 'The Mirrour of Knighthood,' *The Romanic Review*, 4 (1913), pp. 397–402.

20 Although diplomatic and commercial ties between England and Spain had existed ever since the days of Catherine of Aragon, it was not until the defeat of the Armanda in 1588 that Spanish as a language gained some currency. Prior to that time even Spanish dictionaries seem to have been rare. See John Underhill, *Spanish Literature in the England of the Tudors* (London: Macmillan, 1899), esp. pp. 328–38, 228–59.

21 Prior to Tyler's work only a few chivalric romances (translated from the French or the Italian versions) had been available in English. Tyler's *Mirrour* was so successful commercially that the same printer, Thomas East, soon commissioned the translation of *The Second Part of the Mirrour of Knighthood* (1583). The translator of this second part was one R.P. (Robert Parry), as Tyler was probably too old for another laborious translating task. The series continued to be translated until 1601, when the whole work was completed in eight volumes. The Spanish originals of the *Mirrour* were written by four different authors between 1562 and 1589. See R.S. Crane, *The Vogue of Medieval Chivalric Romance During the English Renaissance* (Menasha, Wisconsin, 1919), p. 16.

22 Henry Thomas discusses the relationship of the *Mirrour* to other chivalric romances in his book *Spanish and Portuguese Romances of Chivalry* (Cambridge: Cambridge University Press, 1920).

23 See Dorothy Atkinson, 'Busirane's Castle and Artidon's Cave,' *Modern Language Quarterly*, 1 (1940), pp. 185–92; J. Perott, 'The probable source of Shakespeare's *Tempest*,' *Publications of the Clark University Library*, 1 (1905), pp. 209–16; and Harold Golder, 'Bunyan's Valley of the Shadow,' *Modern Philology*, 27 (1929), pp. 55–72.

24 In *First Feminists*, already cited, Moira Ferguson states that Tyler's Preface is 'the first explicitly feminist argument published by a woman . . . in English,' p. 52.

25 See E.D. Mackerness, 'Margaret Tyler: an Elizabethan feminist,' *Notes and Queries*, 190.6 (1946), pp. 112–13; Betty Travitsky (ed.), op. cit. pp. 144–6; and Moira Ferguson (ed.), op. cit., pp. 51–7.

26 Textual material here and throughout is taken from the 1578 British Museum copy of *The Mirrour*, cited above.

27 In *A mirrhor mete for all mothers, Matrones and Maidens* (London, 1579).

28 The first meaning, now obsolete, that the *OED* gives of the word 'story' is: 'A narrative, true or presumed to be true, relating to important events and celebrated persons of a more or less remote past; a historical relation or anecdote.' From the phrasing of the full title of *Mirrour*, it would appear that Tyler is using the word in this sense.

29 This last sentence calls to mind Chaucer's comment in the opening of *The Book of the Duchess*, where he describes himself as lying awake and asking for 'a romance to rede and drive away a wery night.'

30 Lawrence Stone, *The Family, Sex and Marriage* (London: Weidenfeld & Nicolson, 1977), p. 193.

31 R. Kelso, *Doctrine for the Lady of the Renaissance* (Urbana: University of Illinois Press, 1956), p. 94.

32 Barbara Louise Magaw, 'The female characters in prose chivalric romances in England 1475–1603,' Ph.D. dissertation, University of Maryland (1973), p. 58.

33 Magaw concurs, ibid., p. 89.

34 About the Penelope and Griselda theme in recreational literature addressed to women, see Suzanne Hull, *Chaste, Silent and Obedient: English Books for Women, 1475–1640* (San Marino, California: Huntington Library, 1982), p. 81.

35 That *The Mirrour* prioritizes the issues and draws the attention away from defence as a mere game is evident from an incident in chapter 52, in which a woman demands a defence of her beauty. The Knight of the Sun laughs at her cause, although he finally does what she asks, and the chapter ends with a lesson on misplaced preoccupation with beauty. This is very much unlike the emphasis in many other chivalric romances and in Queen Elizabeth's own court. On 26 February 1588, Cumberland and Essex made challenge that 'they will runne all corners to maintain that the Queen is most worthiest and most fairest Amadis de Gaule.' (Recorded by Miller in *The Professional Writer in Elizabethan England* (Cambridge, Massachusetts: Harvard University Press, 1959), pp. 80–1.)

36 See S. Shepherd, *Amazons and Warrior Women* (Brighton: Harvester Press, 1981), esp. pp. 5–17.

37 Googe translated into English verse some of the passages of Montemayor's prose romance *Diana*. In the process, he toned down dialogues between female characters that sounded too permissive by English standards. Some translators of Italian material carried out similar changes or interjected moral lessons which they addressed directly to female readers.

3 NOBLEWOMEN DRAMATIZING THE HUSBAND–WIFE CONFLICT

1 Ruth Kelso, *Doctrine for the Lady of the Renaissance* (Urbana: University of Illinois Press, 1956), p. 1.

2 Keith Wrightson, *English Society 1580–1680* (New Jersey: Rutgers University Press, 1982), pp. 93, 95. For the arrangement of marriages among propertied classes, see Wrightson, p. 80, and Lawrence Stone, *The Family, Sex and Marriage* (London: Weidenfeld & Nicolson, 1977), p. 87.

3 Her parents viewed the match as an opportunity for social advancement, as we can gather from the letter of Sir Henry Sidney to the Earl of Leicester – see Frances Young, *Mary Sidney, Countess of Pembroke*

(London: David Nutt, 1912), pp. 28–9. But we have no evidence of young Mary's feelings on the matter.

4 Nicholas Breton says that Mary Herbert's husband was in 'no meane commaund.' A certain codicil that survives from the Earl's will points to some sort of breach between them, but it is impossible to determine the source or nature of the problem, which was apparently resolved before the Earl's death. (See Frances Young, op. cit., pp. 81–2.)

5 For evidence of Mary Herbert's theatrical activity see Josephine Roberts, 'Part II: Mary Sidney, Countess of Pembroke,' *English Literary Renaissance*, 14.3 (1984), p. 426; and Mary Edmond, 'Pembroke's Men,' *Review of English Studies*, 25 (1974), pp. 130–1. In *The Herberts of Wilton* (1967), Sir Tresham Lever mentions that Shakespeare's *As You Like It* was performed at Wilton in 1603.

6 Of these, only the *Discourse* and *Antonie* were published (together in 1592) by Lady Herbert. A couple of her occasional poems appeared in collections by Spenser and Francis Davison. The rest of her work remained unpublished until long after her death. See Gary Waller's edition, *The 'Triumph of Death' and other Unpublished and Uncollected Poems by Mary Sidney, Countess of Pembroke (1561–1621)* (Salzburg: Institut für Englische Sprache und Literatur, 1977), and his study, *Mary Sidney, Countess of Pembroke: A Critical Study of her Writings and Literary Milieu* (Salzburg: Institut für Englische Sprache und Literatur, 1979).

7 Gary Waller examines these changes in *Mary Sidney . . .*, already cited. In a carefully researched essay, Beth Wynne Fisken also examines the revisions of the Psalms and finds that Mary Herbert's constant reworking of image, syntax, and form led to the 'development of a style independent of her brother's influence, reflecting her own ideas, tastes, and experiences'. (See 'Mary Sidney's Psalmes: education and wisdom,' in M. Hannay (ed.), *Silent But for the Word* (Kent, Ohio: Kent State University Press, 1986), p. 169.)

8 Mary Ellen Lamb, 'The Countess of Pembroke's patronage,' *English Literary Renaissance*, 12.2 (1982), pp. 167–73.

9 ibid., p. 168.

10 Quoted by Waller in *Mary Sidney . . .* , pp. 41–2.

11 M.E. Lamb, op. cit., p. 170.

12 ibid., pp. 175–6.

13 Alice Luce, the first modern editor of *Antonie*, made a useful comparison between Garnier's original text and the Countess's translation and found that Lady Herbert stuck to the original even at the occasional expense of awkward rendering – see *The Countess of Pembroke's Antonie* (Literarhistorische Forschungen, 1987). This is apparently not the case with her translations of more solemn subjects. Diane Bornstein analyses the Countess's Englishing of Mornay's *Discourse of Life and Death* and concludes that the English text is a faithful but skilful and idiomatic rendering of the original: 'The style of the Countess of Pembroke's translation of Philippe de Mornay's *Discours de la vie et*

de la mort,' in M. Hannay (ed.), *Silent But for the Word,* p. 134.

14 Mary Ellen Lamb, 'The myth of the Countess of Pembroke: the dramatic circle,' *Yearbook of English Studies*, 11 (1981), pp. 195–202.

15 For the difference between Senecan and neo-Senecan traditions in France, Italy, and England see T.S. Eliot, 'Seneca in Elizabethan translation,' in *Selected Essays* (London: Faber & Faber, 1932), esp. p. 83; and 'Senecan tradition in England,' in *The Political Works of Sir William Alexander*, vol. I, ed. L.E. Kastner and H.B. Charlton, (London: Blackwood, 1921), esp. pp. 163–85.

16 See Mary Morrison, 'Some aspects of the treatment of the theme of Antony and Cleopatra in tragedies of the sixteenth century,' *Journal of European Studies*, 4 (1974), pp. 113–25; and Max Patrick, 'The Cleopatra theme in world literature up to 1700,' in J.R.C. Perkin (ed.), *The Undoing of Babel* (Toronto: McClelland & Stewart, 1975), pp. 64–76.

17 Textual citations here and throughout refer to Geoffrey Bullough's edition of *Antonie* in *Narrative and Dramatic Sources of Shakespeare,* vol. V (Princeton: Princeton University Press, 1981).

18 *The Tragedy of Cleopatra*, Act I, ll. 67–70.

19 M. Morrison, op. cit., p. 120.

20 *The Prince*, trans. W.K. Marriott (London and Toronto: Dent & Dutton, 1908), p. 134.

21 For Daniel's Cleopatra, motherly feeling comes last, despite the fact that her children figure dramatically in the play.

22 Alexander Witherspoon, *The Influence of Robert Garnier* (New York: Archon Books, 1924, rpt. 1968), pp. 8–9.

23 Betty Travitsky (ed.), *The Paradise of Women* ... (Westport, Connecticut: Greenwood Press, 1981), p. 9.

24 See Jonathan Dollimore, *Radical Tragedy: Religion, Ideology and Power in the Drama of Shakespeare and His Contemporaries* (Brighton: Harvester Press, 1984).

25 Daniel was suspected of involvement in the Essex rebellion on account of his *Philotas*. He vehemently denied any connection, but the fact is that his play was interpreted differently by Elizabeth's censoring authorities.

26 Lady Joanna Lumley had translated Euripides' play *Iphigenia at Aulis* around 1550, when she was a young teenager. But she never published her work, which appears to have been a classroom exercise. It was edited by Harold Child and printed for the Malone Society in 1909.

27 *The Muses Sacrifice or Divine Meditations* (London: G. Norton, 1612), sig. 2r. Davies devotes four stanzas to the praise of Elizabeth Cary. In them he alludes to her dramatic compositions and her rare talents as a woman writer. Among other things he says:

> Thou mak'st Melpomen proud, and my Heart great
> of such a Pupill, who, in Buskin fine,
> With Feete of State, dost make thy Muse to mete

the Scenes of Syracuse and Palestine

....

Such nervy Limbes of Art, and Straines of Wit
   Times past ne'er knew the weaker Sexe to have;

And Times to come, will hardly credit it
   if thus thou give thy Works both Birth and Grave.
                                           (Sig. 3v)

28 When she was twelve, he gave her John Calvin's *Institutes* to read, expecting that she would be baffled, but Elizabeth criticized the Swiss reformer, pointing to flaws and contradictions in his arguments. 'This girl hath a spirit adverse from Calvin,' her father is said to have exclaimed.

29 Georgiana Fullerton, *The Life of Elizabeth Lady Falkland 1585–1639* (London: Burns & Oates, 1883), pp. 1–15.

30 ibid., p. 16.

31 From Sir John Davies's allusion (see n. 27 above) we understand that in addition to *Mariam*, Cary had written another play which was set in Syracuse and which is apparently no longer extant. Her daughter records the composition of yet another work, 'the Life of Tamburlaine in verse,' also not extant. See R. [Richard] S. [Simpson] (ed.), *The Lady Falkland, her Life from a ms. in the Imperial Archives at Lisle* (purported to have been written by her daughter) (London: Catholic Publishing & Bookselling Co., 1861), p. 9.

32 This was in 1626. Her friend, Lady Denbigh, tried to prevent the conversion from taking place, but Lady Cary outwitted her and accomplished her purpose in the stable of her friend's house. Lady Denbigh immediately informed her brother, Duke of Buckingham, and the whole affair became known. Lady Cary's husband, then in Ireland as Lord Deputy, was highly angered and ordered his servants to cut off all supplies from his wife. Lady Cary was reduced to poverty but refused to recant. She petitioned to the king and to members of the Privy Council for support. She was finally reconciled to her husband after about a two-year period through the intervention of the queen, the Catholic Henrietta-Maria. These facts are gathered from the two biographies already cited (the daughter's account and Fullerton's) and also from Kenneth Murdock's biographical essay in *The Sun at Noon: Three Biographical Sketches* (New York: Macmillan, 1939).

33 *The Famous and Memorable Workes of Josephus* (London: Printed for G. Bishop and others, 1602). If Cary wrote the play before Lodge's translation was published, she could have used a manuscript copy of it. (Her friend Drayton was also one of Lodge's close friends.) And in any case, she could have gone to the French and Latin versions from which Lodge translated. She appears to have relied mainly on the *Antiquities*, chapters 15 and 16, but has also used some material from *Wars*. See Dunstan's introduction in the Malone Society reprint of *Mariam* (London: Charles Whittingham, 1914), pp. xiv–xv.

34 See Maurice Valency, *The Tragedies of Herod and Mariamne* (New York: Columbia University Press, 1940). The list of plays acted and/or printed in the English Renaissance includes: Cary's *The Tragedy of Mariam*, (1613); Markham and Sampson's *Herod and Antipater* (1620, 1622); and Massinger's *The Duke of Milan* (1623).

35 This is also a point noted by Travitsky in her essay, 'The *feme covert* in Elizabeth Cary's *Mariam*,' in C. Levin and J. Watson (eds), *Ambiguous Realities* (Detroit: Wayne State University Press, 1987).

36 Here and throughout, line numbers for quoted material refer to the Malone Society reprint of *The Tragedie of Mariam, The Faire Queene of Jewry* (London: Charles Whittingham, 1914).

37 Catherine Belsey, *The Subject of Tragedy: Identity and Difference in Renaissance Drama* (London and New York: Methuen, 1985), p. 173.

38 *The Famous and Memorable Workes of Josephus*, trans. Thomas Lodge (London, 1602), pp. 397, 398.

39 Leonora Brodwin, *Elizabethan Love Tragedy 1587–1625* (New York: New York University Press, 1971), p. 185.

40 Valency, op. cit., p. 279.

41 Belsey sees this as a conflict between liberal humanism and Elizabethan notions of absolutist marriage (*The Subject of Tragedy . . .*, p. 174).

42 ibid., p. 173.

43 Nancy Cotton Pearse has suggested that Salome represents Cary's own rebellious self, as evidenced by her activities after her conversion to Catholicism. See 'Elizabeth Cary, Renaissance playwright,' *Texas Studies in Literature and Language*, 18 (Winter 1977), p. 605.

44 B. Travitsky, 'The *feme covert . . .*,' p. 192.

45 The daughter purported to have written her mother's biography states that the play was stolen out of her mother's drawer – see R. [Richard] S. [Simpson], op. cit., p. 9; G. Fullerton, op. cit., p. 16. Although there appears to be nothing surreptitious about the play's entry in the Stationer's Register, the daughter's comment is still interesting as a description of her mother's attitude.

46 See Donald Stauffer, 'A deep and sad passion,' in H. Craig (ed.), *The Parrott Presentation Volume* (Princeton: Princeton University Press, 1935), esp. pp. 300–11.

47 The full title of the British Museum copy of this volume is, *The History of The Life, Reign, and Death of Edward II. King of England, and Lord of Ireland. With The Rise and Fall of his great Favourites, Gaveston and the Spencers. Written by E.F. in the year 1627. And Printed Verbatim from the Original* (London: J.C. for Charles Harper et al., 1680), STC 313.

48 *The History of the most unfortunate Prince King Edward II. With Choice Political Observations on Him and his unhappy Favourites, Gaveston and Spencer* (London: A.G. and J.P., 1680), STC 314. The authenticity of this shorter version has been called into question, mainly by Donald Stauffer who thinks it is the printer's condensed version of the longer work. Curiously, the two printers do not seem to

have read very carefully the manuscripts they printed; if they did, they chose to ignore an overwhelming part of the evidence that contradicted their prejudices and purposes. In his address to the reader, the publisher of the folio volume praises the history for its 'so Masculine a stile' (sig. A2r), while the publisher of the octavo even attempts to present the history as a favourable account of Edward II. He cites contemporary critics whose opinions contradict the facts in the Falkland history and, finding that 'Our author closes his History without declaring the particulars of the Murder of this Prince' (A3r), he supplies these particulars from the version of one Richard Baker! The fact that he supplies them in the preface, however, is perhaps an indication that he did not tamper with the text too much.

49 D.A. Stauffer, op. cit., pp. 294–314. See also Tina Krontiris, 'Style and gender in Elizabeth Cary's *Edward II*,' in A. Haselkorn and B. Travitsky (eds), *The Englishwoman in Print* (Amherst: University of Massachusetts Press, 1990), pp. 137–40.

50 The list would include: Fabyan, Grafton, Holinshed, Stow, Speed, Hardyng, Marlowe, Shakespeare, and Drayton. The last one, who had been Lady Falkland's tutor when she was young, took up the subject repeatedly. In 1928 one Francis Hubert or Hobert published a poem on 'The Deplorable Life and Death of Edward the Second' (D.A. Stauffer, op. cit., p. 299).

51 See D.A. Stauffer, op. cit., p. 309.

52 Marlowe was apparently the first to introduce Edward's attitude of neglect towards the queen (see R.S. Knox's introduction to his edition of *Edward II* (London: Methuen, 1923), pp. 14–15).

53 The basic notion she expresses is that the king 'should on earth order his proceedings in imitation after the Divine Nature' (p. 140). The subjects are justified in rebelling when the king tyrannizes over them.

54 This is also Stauffer's view (op. cit., p. 301).

55 Unless otherwise indicated, page numbers given in parentheses will refer to the folio edition, which is the text I have mainly relied on in this study. The octavo volume I occasionally cite is the 1680 edition.

56 We do not know what Lady Cary's intentions were with respect to publication, but the very presence of a reader's preface suggests that an audience, if not immediately sought, was at least in the back of her mind.

57 The octavo reads: 'The King grows sad and melancholly, calling to mind the Injustice of his own Actions, and the fair Cause his Wife had to seek her right and refuge. The neglect and breach of Wedlock was so great an Error, but so to contemn so sweet and great a Queen, was a fault, in his own thoughts, deserv'd a heavy censure' (pp. 39–40).

58 It is likely that Lady Falkland recognized something of her own experience in this. We know that to achieve her conversion to Catholicism she had to dissemble and to carry out her plans secretly.

59 Fullerton, op. cit., p. 29.

60 *The Reply of the Most Illustrious Cardinall of Perron, to the . . . King of Great Britaine* (Dovay: Martin Bogart, 1630), sig. A2v.

4 WOMEN OF THE JACOBEAN COURT DEFENDING THEIR SEX

1 Retha Warnicke, *Women of the English Renaissance and Reformation* (Westport, Connecticut: Greenwood Press, 1983), p. 208.

2 There seems to be a wide range of opinion about whether or not Jacobean dramatists opposed or championed women's traditional roles, with Lisa Jardine (*Still Harping on Daughters*) and Linda Woodbridge (*Women and the English Renaissance*) representing the pessimistic and optimistic sides respectively. Most critics agree that Webster's plays do at least question traditional values on gender.

3 A.L. Rowse (ed.), *The Poems of Shakespeare's Dark Lady: Salve Deus Rex Judaeorum by Emilia Lanyer* (London: Jonathan Cape, 1978), pp. 11–12. As the title indicates, Rowse tries to prove that Lanyer was the 'Dark Lady' of Shakespeare's sonnets. He thus most unfortunately deflects the attention from Lanyer as an author. But his work is useful in that it provides us with an accessible edition of her poetry and gathers together into a kind of biography all that is known about Lanyer's life, mainly from the records of Forman the astrologer, whom Lanyer visited several times.

4 Cited in A.L. Rowse (ed.), op. cit., p. 12.

5 B. Travitsky (ed.), *The Paradise of Women: Writings by Englishwomen of the Renaissance* (Westport, Connecticut: Greenwood Press, 1981), p. 29.

6 A.L. Rowse (ed.), op. cit., p. 53. I have used as primary text the British Library copy of *Salve Deus Rex Judaeorum* (London: Valentine Simmes for Richard Bonian, 1611), but for material omitted from that copy, as in this instance, I have relied on Rowse's edition. Signatures and page numbers respectively refer to these two sources.

7 Our main sources of biographical information on Lady Margaret Clifford, Countess of Cumberland, include her long biographical letter to Dr Layfield (reprinted in George C. Williamson, *George, Third Earl of Cumberland, 1558–1605: His Life and His Voyages* (Cambridge: Cambridge University Press, 1920), pp. 285–8) and the accounts of her daughter, Lady Anne Clifford, in the latter's *Diary* and *Lives* of her parents.

8 George Clifford, Third Earl of Cumberland, seaman, adventurer, and womanizer, was separated from his wife, Lady Margaret, for several years in the last part of his life. They were finally reconciled on his deathbed, but apparently not soon enough for Lady Margaret to have exerted any influence when he made his will (eleven days before his death on 30 October 1605), in which he bequeathed his northern estates to his brother, Sir Francis Clifford. On the basis of an old deed that entailed the family estates upon her husband's child regardless of sex, the dowager

Countess initiated court proceedings and collected documents in support of her daughter's claim.

9 G.C. Williamson, op. cit., p. 295.

10 Jonson's 'To Sir Robert Wroth' (published in *The Forest*, 1616) is usually cited as the first English original composition in praise of a life in the country, away from the turbulence of the city and the court. But epigrams on the court and the country had appeared as early as 1600. See Maren-Sofie Rostvig, *The Happy Man: Studies in the Metamorphoses of a Classical Ideal*, vol. I (Oslo: Norwegian Universities Press, 1962), esp. pp. 55–67.

11 See Mary Ellen Lamb, 'The Countess of Pembroke's patronage,' *English Literary Renaissance*, 12.2 (1982), pp. 162–79.

12 Although Lanyer's interest in religion must be taken as granted, the extent of her conversion (hinted at in the opening of her 'Description of Cooke-ham') must be questioned. Certainly, if the conversion she vaguely alludes to did take place, the effect of religious thought on her intellectual development cannot have been as profound as, say, that of Lady Cary or Lady Pembroke.

13 Cited in A.L. Rowse (ed.), op. cit., p. 12.

14 This would seem to be a Catholic rather than a Protestant concept, but in its context it does not appear to have a specifically religious meaning. It is most likely a reference to Lady Cumberland's preoccupation with philanthropy. Her husband's biographer tells us that she engaged in works of social welfare. One of her greatest projects was the construction of a boarding house for poor women. She also interested herself in prisoners in Fleet Street. See George Williamson, op. cit., esp. pp. 290–6.

15 Caroline Walker Bynum, 'The Body of Christ in the Later Middle Ages: a reply to Leo Steinberg,' *Renaissance Quarterly*, 39 (Autumn 1986), pp. 411–37.

16 Margaret Walters, 'The naked Christian,' in *The Male Nude: A New Perspective* (New York and London: Paddington Press, 1978), p. 77.

17 Quoted in C. Walker Bynum, op. cit., p. 417.

18 Barbara Lewalski sees an attempt on the part of Lanyer to create a community of Good Women, 'fusing religious devotion and feminism so as to assert the essential harmony of these two impulses'. See 'Of God and good women: the poems of Aemilia Lanyer,' in M. Hannay (ed.), *Silent But for the Word* (Kent, Ohio: Kent State University Press, 1985), p. 207. Elaine Beilin does not find a feminist spirit in the poem. Instead, she sees Lanyer's praise of women as evolving 'from her own piety and her poetic calling as a Christian visionary who yearns for a world greatly different from the one she knows' – see *Redeeming Eve: Women Writers of the English Renaissance* (Princeton: Princeton University Press, 1987), p. 181.

19 Barbara Lewalski suggests that it is. See 'Of God and good women . . .', p. 220.

20 The removal of the dedication to Arabella Stuart is the only one that can be easily explained, for 1611 was the year of her final disgrace.

Although her secret marriage to William Seymour (which would strengthen her claim to the English throne) was discovered not long after it took place in early July 1610 (before Lanyer's book was registered), Arabella's continued efforts to escape the king's orders that placed her under confinement, and her final attempt on 4 July 1611 to sail secretly to France, resulted in her final condemnation and commitment to the Tower. Lady Katherine, wife of Thomas Howard, Lord Admiral and Lord Chamberlain of the Household, was the only other controversial figure among the dedicatees whose names were removed. She and her husband used state funds for building their luxurious manor. They were imprisoned for extortion and embezzlement. But this did not occur until 1618.

21 *Love's Victorie* was never published and is currently in private hands.

22 Mary Wroth, *The Poems of Lady Mary Wroth*, ed. Josephine Roberts (Baton Rouge: Louisiana State University Press, 1983), p. 40. This is a very carefully prepared edition with an introduction and a short biography. I have relied on it extensively.

23 Carolyn Swift, 'Feminine identity in Lady Mary Wroth's romance *Urania*,' *English Literary Renaissance*, 14.3 (1984), p. 332.

24 Both her trips abroad and her experiences at court were likely to have a strong influence on Mary Wroth's writing. Court life certainly provided her with rich source material for her romance.

25 In 'To Lady Mary Wroth' Jonson writes:

> Know you to be a Sydney, though un-nam'd?
> And, being nam'd, how little doth that name
> Need any Muses praise to give it fame?

Jonson dedicated to Lady Mary two other poems and his *Alchemist*. He also exscribed her sonnets, a task which, he claimed, made him 'A Better lover, and a much better Poet' (*Underwood*, xxviii).

26 Quoted by Roberts in *Poems*, p. 19.

27 Copied from the British Library edition of the *Urania*. May Nelson Paulissen also calls attention to this announcement as display of literary heritage, *The Sonnets of Lady Mary Wroth: A Critical Introduction* (Salzburg: Institut für Englische Sprache und Literatur, 1982), p. 1.

28 For discussions of Mary Wroth's poetry see Josephine Roberts's introduction to *Poems*; her article, 'Lady Mary Wroth's sonnets: a labyrinth of the mind,' *Journal of Women's Studies in Literature*, 1.4 (1979), pp. 319–29; and her review of Garry Waller's edition, *Lady Mary Wroth: Pamphilia to Amphilanthus*, in *Seventeenth Century News*, 36 (1978), pp. 59–60. Also see Elaine Beilin, '"The Onely Perfect Vertue": Constancy in Mary Wroth's *Pamphilia to Amphilanthus*,' *Spenser Studies*, vol. 2, pp. 229–45; and May Nelson Paulissen, *The Sonnets of Lady Mary Wroth*, already cited.

29 The exact problems are not known, but Jonson's comment, 'my Lady Wroth is unworthily married on a Jealous husband' (recorded in *Conversations with Drummond*), may provide some clue. Also,

husband and wife did not share the same interests. Robert Sidney was not a wealthy man and the 1,000 pounds had been advanced, in the form of a gift, by William Herbert, 3rd Earl of Pembroke, who was ironically to become Lady Mary's greatest passion. See Josephine Roberts, 'The biographical problem of *Pamphilia to Amphilanthus*,' *Tulsa Studies in Women's Literature*, 1 (1982), pp. 43–53.

30 J. Roberts, *Poems*, p. 26.

31 For the source of cited material in this section and for a detailed account of the Denny affair, see Josephine Roberts, 'An unpublished literary quarrel concerning the suppression of Mary Wroth's *Urania*,' *Notes and Queries*, 222 (1977), pp. 532–5; and Paul Salzman, 'Contemporary references to Mary Wroth's *Urania*,' *Review of English Studies*, New Series, 24 (1978), pp. 178–81.

32 Roberts reprints these in the introduction and appendix to *Poems*.

33 C. Swift, op. cit., p. 340.

34 Renaissance readers were in the habit of searching for allusions to actual places and persons in works of fiction. Thus it is not surprising that Wroth's contemporaries would recognize the *Urania* as a satirical *roman-à-clef*.

35 'The death of the heart: Lady Mary Wroth's *Urania*,' in Rosemary Seymour (ed.), *Research Papers '79: Women's Studies* (Hamilton, NZ: Women's Studies Association, 1979), p. 127.

36 Salzman and Roberts both agree that Wroth's denials are unconvincing.

37 Page numbers in parentheses here and throughout will refer to the British Library copy of the 1621 *Urania*.

38 Examples of women in such relationships may be found on pp. 1–11, 436–40, and 472.

39 Roberts too notices Wroth's sensitivity to women's binds and cites the incident she sees as based on the events of the Overbury affair (*Poems*, p. 36).

40 The Earl of Worcester is reported to have said about the queen's ladies: 'the plotting and malice amongst them is such, that I think envy hath tied an invisible snake about most of their necks to sting one another to death.' Quoted by Roberts in *Poems*, p. 27.

41 Carolyn Swift also notes this point ('Feminine identity in Lady Wroth's *Urania*,' p. 334).

42 This may be related to the author's own continental travel experience.

43 Pamphilia's hunting and writing of poetry were not unusual for the Lady of the Jacobean court.

44 Perhaps Wroth's own unhappy marriage fostered this sympathetic attitude.

45 The notion of woman as inconstant, changeable and hysterical was closely linked to prevailing views about the association between the moon and the woman's womb (Greek: *hyster*). A woman was thought to change as a result of the moon's influence over her. Hence screaming and other forms of extreme emotive behaviour

were considered manifestations of that influence. This idea was used to support woman's inconstancy.

46 A similar statement was made by Elizabeth I: 'Yea, to satisfie you, I have already joyned my self in Marriage to an Husband, namely, the Kingdom of England.' Elaine Beilin cites this statement ('Constancy in Mary Wroth's *Pamphilia to Amphilanthus*,' p. 241) and argues that Pamphilia is meant as a parallel to Queen Elizabeth. I have to disagree with Beilin about Pamphilia's constancy to her kingdom and her being a tribute to Queen Elizabeth. Although Beilin is correct in calling attention to the similarities between Pamphilia and Elizabeth, Pamphilia's statement of marriage to her kingdom must be seen in the context of her actions throughout the book.

47 The idea of an Anacreontic Cupid also occurs in Wroth's sonnet sequence, *Pamphilia to Amphilanthus*.

48 For a detailed discussion of the possible meanings of the name Urania, see Graham Parry, 'Lady Mary Wroth's *Urania*,' *Proceedings of the Leeds Philosophical and Literary Society: Literary and History Section*, XVI (1976), pp. 51–5. Parry also suggests the possibility that the name Urania may be Wroth's compliment to her aging aunt, Mary Sidney, Dowager Countess of Pembroke. Mary Sidney died in 1621, shortly before the publication of her niece's *Urania*.

49 An interesting reading of the sonnets in relation to Pamphilia's psychic conflict and the refusal to give in may be found in chapter 4 of Ann Jones's recent study, *The Currency of Eros: Women's Love Lyric in Europe, 1540–1620* (Bloomington: Indiana University Press, 1990).

50 J. Roberts, *Poems*, p. 44.

51 ibid., p. 49.

52 Wroth's unpublished play, *Love's Victorie*, also deals with the theme of love.

53 See Janice Radway, *Reading the Romance: Women, Patriarchy, and Popular Literature* (Chapel Hill: University of North Carolina Press, 1984), chapter 6.

54 Pamphilia and Amphilanthus are first cousins, and the affair is kept secret.

BIBLIOGRAPHY

PRIMARY SOURCES

Anon., *Calendar of State Papers, Domestic Series, 1627–1628*, London: Longman Green, Brown, 1858. (Contains documents relating to Lady Cary and her family.)

Anon., *Calendar of State Papers Relating to Ireland, of the Reign of Charles I, 1625–1632*, London: Her Majesty's Stationery Office, 1900. (Contains documents relating to Lady Cary and her family.)

Cary, Elizabeth, Lady Falkland, *The History of The Life, Reign, and Death of Edward II . . . Printed Verbatim from the Original*, London: J.C. for Charles Harper, Samuel Crouch, and Thomas Fox, 1680.

—— *The History of the most unfortunate Prince King Edward II*, London: A.G. and J.P., 1680. Reprinted with minor alterations in *The Harleian Miscellany: or a Collection of Scarce, Curious, and Entertaining Pamphlets and Tracts*, vol. I, London: printed for T. Osborne, 1744; rpt. 1808.

—— *The Tragedie of Mariam. The Faire Queene of Jewry*, London: Thomas Creede for Richard Hawkins, 1613. Reprinted by the Malone Society with an introduction by A.C. Dunstan and W.W. Greg., London, 1914.

—— *The Reply of the Most Illustrious Cardinall of Perron, to the . . . King of Great Britaine*, Dovay: Martin Bogart, 1630.

Castiglione, Baldassare, *The Book of the Courtier*, trans. Sir Thomas Hoby, London and New York: Dent & Sons, Dutton & Co., 1928.

Clifford, Lady Anne, *Diary*, ed. V. Sackville-West, London: W. Heinemann, 1923.

—— *Lives of Lady Anne Clifford . . . and her Parents*, ed. J.P. Gilson, London: Roxburghe Club, 1916.

Daniel, Samuel, *The Tragedie of Cleopatra*. Reprinted in G. Bullough (ed.), *Narrative and Dramatic Sources of Shakespeare*, vol. V, London: Routledge & Kegan Paul, 1964.

Davies, Sir John, *The Muses Sacrifice or Divine Meditations*, London: G. Norton, 1612. (Includes an interesting dedication to three prominent women.)

Herbert, Mary, Countess of Pembroke (trans.), *The Tragedie of Antonie.*

Doone into English by the Countesse of Pembroke, London: P.S. for W. Ponsonby, 1595. Reprinted in G. Bullough (ed.), *Narrative and Dramatic Sources of Shakespeare*, vol. V, London: Routledge & Kegan Paul, 1964.

Historical Manuscripts Commission, *Report on the manuscripts of Lord De L'Isle and Dudley preserved at Penshurst Place*, 6 vols, London: 1925–66. (Documents pertaining to the Sidney family.)

Hoby, Lady Margaret, *The Diary of Lady Margaret Hoby 1599–1605*, ed. Margaret Meads, London: Routledge & Son, 1930.

Jonson, Ben, *Poems of Jonson*, ed. George Johnston, London: Routledge & Kegan Paul, 1954. (Includes 'To Sir Robert Wroth' and other poems in connection with Lady Wroth.)

Lanyer, Aemilia, *Salve Deus Rex Judaeorum*, London: Valentine Simmes for Richard Bonian, 1611. Reprinted in *The Poems of Shakespeare's Dark Lady*, ed. A.L. Rowse, New York: Clarksone N. Potter, 1979.

Lodge, Thomas (trans.), *The Famous and Memorable Workes of Josephus*, London, 1602.

Lumley, Joanna (trans.), *Iphigenia at Aulis*, ed. Harold Child, London: The Malone Society, 1909.

Machiavelli, Nicolo, *The Prince*, trans. W.K. Marriott, London and New York: Dent & Sons, Dutton & Co., 1980.

Marston, John, *The Workes of Mr J. Marston*, London: Printed for W. Sheares, 1633. (Contains a relevant dedicatory letter to Lady Cary.)

More, Sir Thomas, *St Thomas More: Selected Letters*, ed. Elizabeth Rogers, New Haven and London: Yale University Press, 1961.

Panofsky, Richard (ed.), *The Floures of Philosophie (1572) by Hugh Plat and A Sweet Nosegay (1573) and The Copy of a Letter (1567) by Isabella Whitney*, Delmar, New York: Scholars' Facsimilies and Reprints, 1982.

Shepherd, Simon (ed.), *The Women's Sharp Revenge: Five Women's Pamphlets from the Renaissance*, London: Fourth Estate, 1985.

Speght, Rachel, *Mortalities Memorandum, with a Dreame Prefixed*, London: Edward Griffin for Jacob Bloome, 1621.

Travitsky, Betty (ed.), *The Paradise of Women: Writings by Englishwomen of the Renaissance*, Westport, Connecticut: Greenwood Press, 1981.

Tyler, Margaret (trans.), *The Mirrour of Princely deedes and Knighthood*, London: T. East, 1578.

Whitney, Geoffrey, *A Choice of Emblems*, ed. Henry Green, London: Lovell Reeve, 1866; rpt. 1967.

Whitney, Isabella, *The Copy of a letter, lately written in meeter by yonge Gentilwoman: to her unconstant Lover*, London: Richard Jones, 1567(?).

—— *A Sweet Nosegay, or pleasant Posye*, London: Richard Jones 1573.

—— 'The Wyll and Testament of Isabella Whitney,' ed. Betty Travitsky, *English Literary Renaissance* 10 (1980), pp. 76–94.

Wroth, Mary, *The Poems of Lady Mary Wroth*, ed. Josephine Roberts, Baton Rouge: Louisiana University Press, 1983.

—— *The Countesse of Montgomeries Urania*, London: John Marrot and John Grismand, 1621.

—— *Pamphilia to Amphilanthus*, ed. Gary Waller, Salzburg Studies in English Literature, Salzburg: Institut für Englische Sprache und Literatur, 1977.

MODERN EDITIONS AND ANTHOLOGIES OF WOMEN'S TEXTS

Cary, Elizabeth, *The Tragedie of Mariam, The Faire Queene of Jewry*. For the Malone Society, ed. A.C. Dunstan and W.W. Greg, with an introduction, London, 1914 (A reprint of the 1613 edn).

—— *The Tragedy of Mariam*, ed. Margaret Ferguson, (forthcoming).

Clifford, Lady Anne, *The Diary of Lady Anne Clifford*, ed. V. Sackville-West, London: William Heinemann, 1923.

Elizabeth Tudor, Queen of England, *Poems of Queen Elizabeth I*, ed. Leicester Bradner, Providence, R.I.: Brown University Press, 1964.

Ferguson, Moira (ed.), *First Feminists: British Women Writings 1578–1799*, Bloomington: Indiana University Press 1986. (Includes Tyler's Dedication and Preface to *Mirrour* and feminist tracts by Anger and Sowernam.)

Herbert, Mary, Countess of Pembroke (trans.), '*The Triumph of Death*' *and Other Unpublished and Uncollected Poems*, ed. Gary Waller, Salzburg: Institut für Englische Sprache and Literatur, 1977.

—— (trans.), '*The Triumph of Death*' *Translated out of the Italian by the Countess of Pembroke*, ed. Frances Young, PMLA 27 (1912), pp. 47–75.

—— (trans.), *The Tragedie of Antonie*, in G. Bullough (ed.), *Narrative and Dramatic Sources of Shakespeare*, vol. I, London: Routledge & Kegan Paul, 1964.

—— (trans.), *The Countess of Pembroke's Translation of Philippe de Mornay's Discourse of Life and Death*, ed. Diane Bornstein, Detroit: Medieval and Renaissance Monographs, 1983.

—— (trans.), *The Psalms of Sir Philip Sidney and the Countess of Pembroke*, ed. J.C.A. Rathmell, New York: Anchor Books, 1963.

Hoby, Lady Margaret, *The Diary of Lady Hoby*, ed. Dorothy Meads, London: Routledge & Sons, 1930.

Lanyer, Aemilia, *The Poems of Shakespeare's Dark Lady*, ed. A.L. Rowse, New York: Clarksone N. Potter, 1979.

Lumley, Joanna (trans.), *Iphigenia at Aulis*, ed. Harold Child, London: The Malone Society, 1909.

Shepherd, Simon (ed.), *The Women's Sharp Revenge: Five Women's Pamphlets from the Renaissance*, London: Fourth Estate, 1985. (Includes feminist tracts by Jane Anger, Rachel Speght, Ester Sowernam, Constantia Munda, and Mary Tattlewell.)

Travitsky, Betty (ed.), *The Paradise of Women: Writings by Englishwomen of the Renaissance*, Westport, Connecticut: Greenwood Press, 1981. (Contains small excerpts from a wide range of writings.)

Whitney, Isabella, *The Floures of Philosophie (1572) by Sir Hugh Plat and A Sweet Nosegay (1573) and The Copy of a Letter (1567) by Isabella Whitney*, ed. Richard Panofsky, Delmar, N.Y.: Scholars' Facsimiles and Reprints, 1982.

—— 'The Wyll and Testament of Isabella Whitney,' ed. Betty Travitsky, *English Literary Renaissance* 10 (1980), pp. 76–94.

Wroth, Mary, *The Poems of Lady Mary Wroth*, ed. Josephine Roberts, Baton Rouge: Louisiana University Press, 1983.

—— *Pamphilia to Amphilanthus*, ed. Gary Waller, Salzburg: Institut für Englische Sprache und Literatur, 1977.

—— *The Countess of Montgomery's Urania*, ed. Josephine Roberts, (forthcoming)

SECONDARY SOURCES

Adamson, J.W., 'The extent of literacy in England in the fifteenth and sixteenth centuries,' *The Library* 10 (1930), 163–93.

Althusser, Louis, 'Ideology and the state,' in *Lenin and Philosophy and Other Essays*, London: New Left Books, 1977.

Armstrong, Nancy and Tennenhouse, Leonard (eds), *The Ideology of Conduct: Essays on Literature and the History of Sexuality*, London: Routledge, 1987.

Bainton, Rolan, H. 'Learned women in the sixteenth century,' in Patricia Labalme (ed.), *Beyond Their Sex*, New York: New York University Press, 1980.

Ballard, George, *Memoirs of Several Ladies of Great Britain*, ed. Ruth Perry, Detroit: Wayne State University Press, 1985.

Barrett, Michele, 'Ideology and the cultural construction of gender,' in Judith Newton and Deborah Rosenfelt (eds), *Feminist Criticism and Social Change: Sex, Class and Race in Literature and Culture*, London: Methuen, 1985.

Batsleer, Janet *et al.*, *Rewriting English: Cultural Politics of Gender and Class*, London and New York: Methuen, 1985.

Beer, Gillian, *The Romance*, Critical Idiom Series, London and New York: Methuen, 1970.

Beilin, Elaine, '"The Onely perfect vertue": Constancy in Mary Wroth's *Pamphilia to Amphilanthus*,' *Spenser Studies* (2), pp. 229–45.

—— 'Anne Askew's self-portrait in the *Examinations*,' in Margaret Hannay (ed.), *Silent But for the Word*, Ohio: Kent State University Press, 1986.

—— *Redeeming Eve: Women Writers of the English Renaissance*, Princeton: Princeton University Press, 1987.

Bell, Maureen, Parfitt, George, and Shepherd, Simon (eds), *A Biographical Dictionary of English Women Writers 1580–1720*, Sussex: Harvester, 1990.

Belsey, Catherine, *Critical Practice*, London and New York: Methuen, 1980.

—— *The Subject of Tragedy: Identity and Difference in Renaissance Drama*, London and New York: Methuen, 1985.

Bennett, H.S., *English Books and Readers, 1603–1640*, Cambridge: Cambridge University Press, 1970.

Bergeron, David, 'Women as patrons of English Renaissance drama,' in

G.F. Lytle and S. Orgel (eds), *Patronage in the Renaissance*, Princeton: Princeton University Press, 1981.

Brink, J.R. (ed.), *Female Scholars: A Tradition of Learned Women*, Montreal: Eden Press Women's Publications, 1980.

Brodwin, Leonora, *Elizabethan Love Tragedy 1587–1625*, New York: New York University Press, 1971.

Brown, Judith, 'A woman's place was in the home: women's work in Renaissance Tuscany,' in Margaret Ferguson, Maureen Quilligan, and Nancy Vickers (eds), *Rewriting the Renaissance*, Chicago: University of Chicago Press, 1987.

Bullough, Geoffrey (ed.), *Narrative and Dramatic Sources of Shakespeare*, vol. V, Princeton: Princeton University Press, 1981.

Bynum, Caroline Walker, 'The body of Christ in the later Middle Ages: a reply to Leo Steinberg,' *Renaissance Quarterly* 39 (Autumn 1986), pp. 411–37.

Camden, Carroll, *The Elizabethan Woman*, Mamaroneck, NY: Paul Appel Publications, 1975; 1st edn 1951.

Charlton, H.B. 'The Senecan tradition in England,' in *The Poetical Works of Sir William Alexander*, vol. I, ed. L.E. Kastner and H.B. Charlton, London: Blackwood, 1921.

Charlton, Kenneth, *Education in Renaissance England*, London: Routledge & Kegan Paul, 1965.

Clark, Alice, *Working Life of Women in the Seventeenth Century*, London: Routledge & Sons, 1919.

Collinson, Patrick, 'The role of women in the English Reformation illustrated by the life and friendships of Anne Locke,' in G.J. Cuming (ed.), *Studies in Church History*, vol. II, London: Nelson, 1965.

Cotton, Nancy, 'Elizabeth Cary, Renaissance playwright,' *Texas Studies in Literature and Language* 18 (Winter, 1977), pp. 601–8.

—— *Women Playwrights in England c.1363–1750*. London: Bucknell University Press, 1980.

Crane, R.S., *The Vogue of Medieval Chivalric Romance During the English Renaissance*, Menasha, Wisconsin: George Banta Publishing Co., 1919.

Cressy, David, *Education in Tudor and Stuart England*, London: Edward Arnold, 1975.

—— *Literacy and the Social Order: Reading and Writing in Tudor and Stuart England*, Cambridge: Cambridge University Press, 1980.

Culler, Jonathan, *The Pursuit of Signs: Semiotics, Literature, Deconstruction*, London: Routledge & Kegan Paul, 1981.

Davies, Zemon Natalie, *Society and Culture in Early Modern France*, London: Duckworth, 1975.

Dollimore, Jonathan, 'The dominant and the deviant: a violent dialectic,' *Critical Quarterly* 28, nos 1 & 2 (Spring/Summer 1986), pp. 179–92.

—— *Radical Tragedy: Religion, Ideology, and Power in the Drama of Shakespeare and his Contemporaries*, Brighton: Harvester Press, 1984.

—— and Sinfield, Alan (eds), *Political Shakespeare: New Essays in Cultural Materialism*, Manchester: Manchester University Press, 1985.

Drakakis, John (ed.), *Alternative Shakespeares*, London and New York: Methuen, 1985.

Duncan-Jones, Katherine, Review of *Silent But for the Word*, ed. Margaret Hannay, *Times Literary Supplement*, 13 June 1986, p. 636.

Dunstan, A.C., *Examination of Two English Dramas*, Königsberg, Germany: Hartungsche Buchdrückerei, 1908.

Dusinberre, Juliet, *Shakespeare and the Nature of Women*, London: Macmillan Press, 1975.

Eagleton, Mary (ed.), *Feminist Literary Theory: A Reader*, Oxford: Basil Blackwell, 1986.

Eagleton, Terry, *Criticism and Ideology: A Study in Marxist Literary Theory*, London: New Left Books, 1976.

—— *Literary Theory: An Introduction*, Oxford: Basil Blackwell, 1983.

—— *Marxism and Literary Criticism*, London: Methuen, 1976.

Edmond, Mary, 'Pembroke's men,' *Review of English Studies* 25 (1974), pp. 130–1.

Eisenstein, Elizabeth, *The Printing Press as an Agent of Change*, vol. I, Cambridge: Cambridge University Press, 1979.

Eliot, T.S., 'Apology for the Countess of Pembroke,' in *The Use of Poetry and the Use of Criticism*, London: Faber & Faber, 1933.

—— 'Seneca in Elizabethan translation,' in *Selected Essays*, London: Faber & Faber, 1932.

Evans, Adelaide Harris, 'The heroine of Middle English romances,' *Western Reserve University Bulletin*, New Series, 31 (August 1928), pp. 5–43.

Everett, Dorothy, 'A characterization of the English medieval romances,' *Essays and Studies* 15 (1929), pp. 98–121.

Everitt, Alan, 'Social mobility in Early Modern England,' *Past and Present* 33 (1966), pp. 56–73.

Ezell, Margaret, *The Patriarch's Wife: Literary Evidence and the History of the Family*, Chapel Hill: University of North Carolina Press, 1987.

Farnham, Willard, *Shakespeare's Tragic Frontier*, Berkeley: University of California Press, 1963. (Includes discussion of the Countess of Pembroke's *Antonie*.)

Farrell, Kirby, Hageman, Elizabeth, and Kinney, Arthur (eds), *Women in the Renaissance: Selections from English Literary Renaissance*, Amherst, Mass: University of Massachusetts Press, 1988.

Fehrenbach, Robert, 'Isabella Whitney and the popular miscellanies of Richard Jones,' *Cahiers Elizabéthians* 19 (1981), pp. 85–7.

—— 'Isabella Whitney, Sir Hugh Plat, Geoffrey Whitney, and Sister Eldershae,' *English Language Notes* 21 (1983), pp. 7–11.

—— 'A Letter sent by Maides of London (1567),' *English Literary Renaissance* 14.3 (1984), pp. 285–304.

Ferante, Joan, 'The education of women in the Middle Ages,' in Patricia Labalme (ed.), *Beyond Their Sex: Learned Women of the European Past*, New York: New York University Press, 1980.

Ferguson, Margaret, Quilligan, Maureen, and Vickers, Nancy (eds), *Rewriting the Renaissance: The Discourse of Sexual Difference in Early Modern Europe*, Chicago: University of Chicago Press, 1987.

Ferguson, Moira (ed.), *First Feminists: British Women Writers 1578–1799*, Bloomington: Indiana University Press, 1985.

Fischer, Sandra, 'Elizabeth Cary and tyranny, domestic and religious,' in Margaret Hannay (ed.), *Silent But for the Word*, Ohio: Kent State University Press, 1986.

Foucault, Michel, *The History of Sexuality*, (trans.) Robert Hurley, Harmondsworth, Middlesex: Penguin Books, 1984.

—— *Power/Knowledge*, (trans.) Colin Gordon, Brighton: Harvester Press, 1980.

Fullerton, Lady Georgiana, *Life of Elizabeth, Lady Falkland 1585–1639*, London: Burns & Oates, 1883.

Gage, Matilda, *Church and State*, Watertown, Mass.: Persephone Press, 1893; rpt. 1981.

Gardiner, Dorothy, *English Girlhood at School*, Oxford: Oxford University Press, 1929.

George, Margaret, 'From "Goodwife" to "Mistress": the transformation of the female in bourgeois culture,' *Science and Society* 37 (1973), pp. 152–77.

Gilbert, Sandra and Gubar, Susan, *The Madwoman in the Attic: The Woman Writer and the Nineteenth-Century Literary Imagination*, New Haven: Yale University Press, 1979.

Goldberg, Jonathan, 'The politics of Renaissance literature: a review essay,' *English Literary History* 49 (1982), pp. 514–42.

Greaves, Richard, *Society and Religion in Elizabethan England*, Minneapolis: University of Minnesota Press, 1981.

Green, Henry (ed.), *A Choice of Emblems*, London: Lovell Reeve, 1866; rpt. 1967.

Greenblatt, Stephen, *Renaissance Self-Fashioning: From More to Shakespeare*, Chicago and London: University of Chicago Press, 1980.

Greene, G., Lenz, C.R., and Neely, C.T., *The Woman's Part: Feminist Criticism of Shakespeare*, Urbana: University of Illinois Press, 1980.

Griffin, N.E., 'The definition of romance,' *PMLA* 38 (1923), pp. 50–70.

Hall, Stuart, 'Cultural studies: two paradigms,' in Tony Bennett, Graham Martin, Colin Mercer, and Janet Woolacott (eds), *Culture, Ideology and Social Process: A Reader*, London: Open University Press, 1981.

Hannay, Margaret (ed.), *Silent But for the Word: Tudor Women as Patrons, Translators, and Writers of Religious Works*, Ohio: Kent State University Press, 1986.

—— 'Unpublished letters by Mary Sidney: a preliminary report,' *Sidney Newsletter* 4.2 (1983), p. 13.

Haselkorn, Anne and Travitsky, Betty, *The Englishwoman in Print, 1500–1640*, Amherst, Mass.: University of Massachusetts Press, 1990.

Heinemann, Margot, *Puritanism and the Theatre: Thomas Middleton and Opposition Drama under the Early Stuarts*, Cambridge: Cambridge University Press, 1980.

Hill, Christine and Morrison, Mary, *Robert Garnier. Two Tragedies, Hippolyte and Marc Antoine*, London: The Athlone Press, 1975.

Hill, Christopher, *The World Turned Upside Down: Radical Ideas During the English Revolution*, London: Temple Smith, 1972.

—— *Intellectual Origins of the English Revolution*, Oxford: Oxford University Press, 1965.

Hobby, Elaine, *Virtue of Necessity: Englishwomen's Writing 1649–88*, London: Virago Press, 1988.

Hoggart, Richard, *The Uses of Literacy*, Harmondsworth, Middlesex: Penguin Books and Chatto & Windus, 1957.

Hughey Willard, Ruth, 'Cultural interests of women in England, 1524–1640, indicated in the writings of the women,' Ph.D. dissertation, University of Virginia, 1936.

Hull, Suzanne, *Chaste, Silent and Obedient: English Books for Women, 1475–1640*, San Marino, California: Huntington Library, 1982.

Jacobus, Mary (ed.), *Women Writing and Writing About Women*, London: Croom Helm, 1979.

Jardine, Lisa, 'Cultural confusion and Shakespeare's learned heroines,' *Shakespeare Quarterly* 38 (Spring 1987), pp. 1–18.

—— 'The Duchess of Malfi: the representation of women,' in Susanne Kappeler (ed.), *Teaching the Text*, London: Routledge & Kegan Paul, 1983.

—— *Still Harping on Daughters: Women and Drama in the Age of Shakespeare*, Totowa, N.J.: Barnes & Noble, 1983.

Jones, Ann Rosalind, *The Currency of Eros: Women's Love Lyric in Europe, 1540–1620*, Bloomington: Indiana University Press, 1990.

—— 'Nets and bridles: early modern conduct books and sixteenth-century women's lyrics,' in Nancy Armstrong and Leonard Tennenhouse (eds), *The Ideology of Conduct: Female Courtesy Books and Literature from the Middle Ages to the Present Day*, London: Methuen, 1987.

Jordan, Constance, 'Feminism and humanists,' in Margaret Ferguson, Maureen Quilligan, and Nancy Vickers (eds), *Rewriting the Renaissance*, Chicago: University of Chicago Press, 1987.

Jordan, W.K., *Philanthropy in England 1480–1660*, London: Allen & Unwin, 1959.

Jusserand, J., *The English Novel in the Time of Shakespeare*, London: T. Fisher Unwin, 1899.

Kaplan, Cora (ed.), *Aurora Leigh and Other Poems*, London: The Women's Press, 1978.

Kelly-Gadol, Joan, 'Did women have a Renaissance?' in R. Bridenthal and C. Koonz (eds), *Becoming Visible: Women in European History*, Boston: Houghton Mifflin, 1977.

Kelso, Ruth, *Doctrine for the Lady of the Renaissance*, Urbana: University of Illinois Press, 1956.

Kohler, Charlotte, 'Elizabethan woman of letters, the extent of her literary activities,' Ph.D. dissertation, University of Virginia, 1936.

Krontiris, Tina, 'Breaking barriers of genre and gender,' *English Literary Renaissance* 18 (1988), pp. 19–39.

—— 'Style and gender in Elizabeth Cary's *Edward II*,' in A. Haselkorn and B. Travitsky (eds), *The Englishwoman in Print, 1500–1640*, Amherst, Mass.: University of Massachusetts Press, 1990.

Labalme, Patricia (ed.), *Beyond Their Sex: Learned Women of the European Past*, New York: New York University Press, 1980.

Lamb, Mary Ellen, 'The Cooke sisters: attitudes toward learned women in the Renaissance,' in M. Hannay (ed.), *Silent But for the Word*, Ohio: Kent State University Press, 1986.

—— 'The Countess of Pembroke's patronage,' *English Literary Renaissance* 12 (1982), pp. 162–79.

—— 'The myth of the Countess of Pembroke: the dramatic circle,' *Yearbook of English Studies* 11 (1981), pp. 194–202.

Lapham, Ella, 'The industrial status of women in Elizabethan England,' *Journal of Political Economy* 9 (1900–1901), pp. 562–99.

Lasage, Julia, 'One way or another: dialectical, revolutionary, feminist,' *Jump Cut*, 20 May 1979, pp. 20–3.

Laslett, Peter, *The World We Have Lost*, London: Methuen, 1965.

Lewalski, Barbara, 'Of God and good women: the poems of Aemilia Lanyer,' in M. Hannay (ed.), *Silent But for the Word*, Ohio: Kent State University Press, 1986.

Lewis, C.S., *The Allegory of Love*, Oxford: Oxford University Press, 1958.

Luce, Alice, 'The Countess of Pembroke's *Antonie*,' in *Literarhistorische Forschungen*, vol. II, Weimar: Verlag von Emil Felber, 1897. (Contains the earliest modern edition of the play.)

Mackerness, E.D., 'Margaret Tyler: an Elizabethan feminist,' *Notes and Queries* 190 (1946), pp. 112–3.

Maclean, Ian, *The Renaissance Notion of Woman*, Cambridge: Cambridge University Press, 1980.

Magaw, Barbara Louise, 'The female characters in prose chivalric romance in England 1475–1603,' Ph.D. dissertation, University of Maryland, 1973.

Mahl, Mary and Koon, Helene (eds), *The Female Spectator: English Women Writers Before 1800*, Bloomington: Indiana University Press, 1977.

Manning, Brian, *Politics, Religion and the English Civil War*, London: Edward Arnold, 1973. (Contains a chapter on 'The reaction of women.')

Margolis, David, *Novel and Society in Elizabethan England*, London: Croom Helm, 1985.

Marriott, J.A., *The Life and Times of Lucius Cary, Viscount Falkland*, London: Methuen, 1908.

Masek, Rosemary, 'Women in an age of transition,' in Barbara Kanner (ed.), *The Women in England from Anglo-Saxon Times to the Present*, London: Mansell, 1980.

McMullen, Norma, 'The education of English gentlewomen 1540–1640,' *History of Education* 6 (1977), pp. 87–101.

Meyer Spacks, Patricia, *The Female Imagination*, New York: Alfred Knopf, 1975.

Miller, Edwin, *The Professional Writer in Elizabethan England*, Cambridge, Massachusetts: Harvard University Press, 1959.

Mitchell, Juliet, *Woman's Estate*, Harmondsworth, Middlesex: Penguin Books, 1971.

Mitchell, Maria, 'Gender and identity in Philip Sidney's *Arcadia*,' Ph. D. dissertation, University of Sussex, 1985.

Moi, Toril, *Sexual/Textual Politics: Feminist Literary Theory*, London and New York: Methuen, 1985.

Morrison, Mary, 'Some aspects of the treatment of the theme of Antony and Cleopatra in tragedies of the sixteenth century,' *Journal of English Studies* 4 (1974), pp. 113–25.

Murdock, Kenneth, *The Sun at Noon: Three Biographical Sketches*, New York: Macmillan, 1939.

Newdigate, Bernard, *Michael Drayton and His Circle*, Oxford: Basil Blackwell, 1941.

Newton, Judith, and Rosenfelt, Deborah (eds), *Feminist Criticism and Social Change: Sex, Class and Race in Literature*, New York and London: Methuen, 1985.

Parott, Joseph, 'The Mirrour of Knighthood,' *Modern Language Notes* 39 (1924), pp. 441–2.

—— 'The Mirrour of Knighthood,' *The Romanic Review* 4 (1913), pp. 397–402.

Parry, Graham, 'Lady Mary Wroth's *Urania*,' *Proceedings of the Leeds Philosophical and Literary Society: Literary and History Section* 16 (1976), pp. 51–60.

Patrick, J. Max, 'The Cleopatra theme in world literature up to 1700,' in J.R. Conway Perkin (ed.), *The Undoing of Babel: Watson Kirkconnell, the Man and his Work*, Toronto: MacLelland & Stewart, 1975.

Paulissen, May Nelson, *The Love Sonnets of Lady Mary Wroth: A Critical Introduction*, Salzburg Studies in English Literature. Salzburg: Institut für Englische Sprache und Literatur, 1982.

Pawling, Christopher (ed.), *Popular Fiction and Social Change*, London: Macmillan Press, 1984.

Plowden, Alison, *Tudor Women: Queens and Commoners*, London: Weidenfeld & Nicolson, 1979.

Poovey, Mary, *The Proper Lady and the Woman Writer: Ideology as Style in the Works of Mary Wollstonecraft, Mary Shelley and Jane Austen*, Chicago: University of Chicago Press, 1984.

Quaife, G.R., *Wanton Wenches and Wayward Wives: Peasants and Illicit Sex in Early Seventeenth Century England*, London: Croom Helm, 1979.

Radway, Janice, *Reading the Romance: Women, Patriarchy and Popular Literature*, Chapel Hill: University of North Carolina Press, 1984.

Reynolds, Myra, *The Learned Lady in England 1650–1760*, Boston: Houghton Mifflin, 1920.

Roberts, Josephine, 'The biographical problem of *Pamphilia to Amphilanthus*,' *Tulsa Studies in Women's Literature* 1 (1982), p. 51.

—— (ed.), *The Poems of Lady Mary Wroth*, Baton Rouge: Louisiana University Press, 1983.

—— 'Lady Mary Wroth's sonnets: a labyrinth of the mind,' *Journal of Women's Studies in Literature* I (Autumn, 1979), pp. 319–29.

—— 'Part II: Mary Sidney, Countess of Pembroke,' *English Literary Renaissance* 14.3 (1984), pp. 426–37. (This is a bibliographical essay.)

—— Review of *Pamphilia to Amphilanthus* by Mary Wroth, ed. Gary

Waller, *Seventeenth Century News* (36), pp. 59–60.

—— 'An unpublished literary quarrel concerning the suppression of Lady Mary Wroth's *Urania* (1621),' *Notes and Queries* 24 (1977), pp. 534–5.

Rose, Mary Beth (ed.), *Women in the Middle Ages and the Renaissance*, Syracuse: Syracuse University Press, 1986.

Rostvig, Maren-Sofie, *The Happy Man: Studies in the Metamorphoses of a Classical Ideal*, vol. I, Oslo: Norwegian Universities Press, 1962.

Rowbotham, Sheila, *Women, Resistance and Revolution*, Harmondsworth, Middlesex: Penguin Books, 1972.

Rowse, A.L. (ed.), *The Poems of Shakespeare's Dark Lady*, London: Jonathan Cape, 1978.

Russ, Joanna, *How To Suppress Women's Writing*, London: The Women's Press, 1983.

Russel, Conrad, *The Origins of the Civil War*, London: Macmillan Press, 1973.

Salzman, Paul, 'Contemporary references in Mary Wroth's *Urania*,' *Review of English Studies* 29 (1978), pp. 178–81.

Schanzer, Ernest, *The Problem Plays of Shakespeare*, London: Routledge & Kegan Paul, 1963. (Compares attitudes towards Antony and Cleopatra in Shakespeare and Garnier.)

Schochet, Gordon, *Patriarchalism in Political Thought*, Oxford: Basil Blackwell, 1975.

Shepherd, Simon, *Amazons and Warrior Women: Varieties of Feminism in Seventeenth Century Drama*, Brighton: Harvester Press, 1981.

S[impson], R[ichard] (ed.), *The Lady Falkland, her Life from a ms. in the Imperial Archives at Lisle*, London: Catholic Publishing & Bookselling Co., 1861.

Sinfield, Alan, 'Power and ideology: an outline theory and Sidney's *Arcadia*,' *English Literary History* 52 (1985), pp. 261–77.

Slater, Miriam, *Family Life in the Seventeenth Century: The Verneys of Claydon House*, London: Routledge & Kegan Paul, 1984.

Spufford, Margaret, *Small Books and Pleasant Histories: Popular Fiction and Its Readership in Seventeenth Century England*, London: Methuen, 1981.

Stallybrass, Peter, 'The body enclosed: patriarchal territories,' in Margaret Ferguson, Maureen Quilligan, and Nancy Vickers (eds), *Rewriting the Renaissance*, Chicago: University of Chicago Press, 1987.

Stauffer, D.A., 'A deep and sad passion,' in Hardin Craig (ed.), *The Parrott Presentation Volume*, Princeton: Princeton University Press, 1935; rpt. 1967.

Stone, Lawrence, *The Family, Sex and Marriage*, London: Weidenfeld & Nicolson, 1977.

—— Review of Antonia Fraser, *The Weaker Vessel*, and of Mary Prior (ed.), *Women in English Society*, in *The New York Review of Books*, April 1985, pp. 21–2.

—— 'The educational revolution in England, 1560–1640,' *Past and Present* 28 (1964), pp. 41–80.

—— 'Social mobility in England, 1500–1700,' *Past and Present* 33 (1966), pp. 16–55.

Swift, Carolyn Ruth, 'Feminine identity in Lady Mary Wroth's romance *Urania,*' *English Literary Renaissance* 14.3 (1984), pp. 328–46.

Thomas, Henry, *Spanish and Portuguese Romances of Chivalry*, Cambridge: Cambridge University Press, 1920.

Thomas, Keith, 'The changing family,' *The Times Literary Supplement* 21 October 1977, p. 1226.

—— 'Women and the Civil War sects,' in T. Aston (ed.), *Crisis in Europe 1560–1660*, London: Routledge & Kegan Paul, 1965.

Travitsky, Betty, 'The *feme covert* in Elizabeth Cary's *Mariam,*' in C. Levin and J. Watson (eds), *Ambiguous Realities: Women of the Middle Ages and the Renaissance*, Detroit: Wayne State University Press, 1987.

—— 'The lady doth protest: protest in the popular writings of Renaissance Englishwomen,' *English Literary Renaissance* 14 (Autumn 1984), pp. 255–83.

—— '"The Wyll and Testament" of Isabella Whitney,' *English Literary Renaissance* 10 (Winter 1980), pp. 76–83.

Valency, Maurice, *Tragedies of Herod and Mariamne*, New York: Columbia University Press, 1940.

Waller, Gary, *Mary Sidney, Countess of Pembroke: A Critical Study of her Writings and Literary Milieu*, Salzburg Studies in English Literature, Salzburg: Institut für Englische Sprache und Literatur, 1979.

Walters, Margaret, *The Male Nude: a New Perspective*, New York and London: Paddington Press, 1978.

Wandor, Michelene (ed.), *On Gender and Writing*, London, Boston, Melbourne, and Henley: Pandora Press, 1983.

Warnicke, Retha, *Women of the English Renaissance and Reformation*, Westport, Connecticut: Greenwood Press, 1983.

Watt, Ian, *The Rise of the Novel*, London: Chatto & Windus, 1974.

Wayne, Valerie, 'Some sad sentences: Vives' instruction of a Christian woman;' in M. Hannay (ed.), *Silent But for the Word*, Ohio: Kent State University Press, 1986.

Weber, Kurt, *Lucius Cary, Second Viscount Falkland*, New York: Columbia University Press, 1940; rpt. 1967.

Whitherspoon, Alexander, *The Influence of Robert Garnier on Elizabethan Drama*; New Haven: Archon Books, 1924; rpt. 1968.

Wiesner, Merry, 'Women in the sixteenth century: a bibliography,' *Sixteenth-Century Bibliography*, 23 (1983), pp. 1–65.

Williams Morgan, Ethyn, 'Women preachers in the Civil War,' *Journal of Modern History* 1 (1929), pp. 561–9.

Williams, Raymond, *Marxism and Literature*, Oxford: Oxford University Press, 1977.

—— *Politics and Letters: Interviews with New Left Review*, London: Verso Editions, 1979.

Williamson, C. George, *George, Third Earl of Cumberland (1558–1605): His Life and Voyages*, Cambridge: Cambridge University Press, 1920.

Wilson, F.P., 'Some notes on authors and patrons in Tudor and Stuart times,' in J.G. McManaway, G.E. Dawson, and E.E. Willoughby (eds),

Joseph Quincy Adams Memorial Studies, Washington, DC: Shakespeare Folger Library, 1948.

Wilson, Katharina (ed.), *Medieval Women Writers*, Manchester: Manchester University Press, 1984.

Witten-Hannah, Margaret, 'The death of the heart: Lady Mary Wroth's *Urania*,' in Rosemary Seymour (ed.), *Research Papers '79: Women's Studies*, Hamilton, NZ: Women's Studies Association, 1979.

—— 'Lady Mary Wroth's *Urania*: the work and the tradition,' Ph.D. dissertation, University of Auckland, 1978.

Woodbridge, Linda, *Women and the English Renaissance: Literature and the Nature of Womankind, 1540–1620*, Brighton: Harvester Press, 1984.

Woolf, Virginia, *A Room of One's Own*, London: Panther Books, 1977. (First printed by the Hogarth Press in 1929.)

Wright, Louis B., *Middle-Class Culture in Elizabethan England*, London: Methuen, 1935.

—— 'The reading of Renaissance English Women,' *Studies in Philology* 28 (1931), pp. 139–57.

Wrightson, Keith, *English Society, 1580–1680*, New Jersey Rutgers University, Press, 1982.

Wyntjes, Marshall Sherrin, 'Women in the Reformation era,' in R. Bridenthal and C. Koonz (eds), *Becoming Visible: Women in European History*, Boston: Houghton Mifflin, 1977.

Young, Frances, *Mary Sidney, Countess of Pembroke*, London: David Nutt, 1912.

INDEX